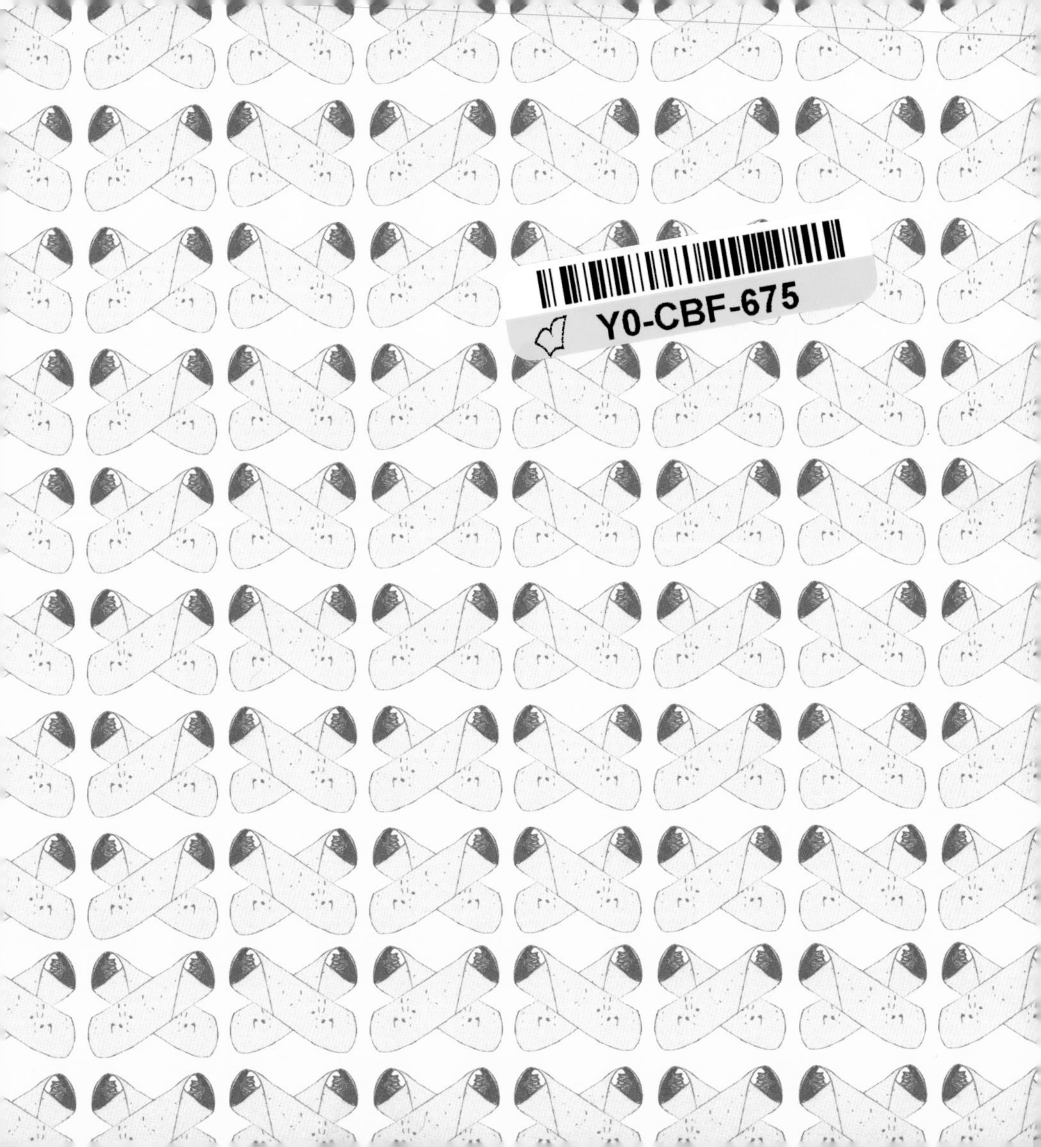

DEFENSIVE EATING WITH MORRISSEY

Vegan Recipes from the One You Left Behind

DEFENSIVE EATING WITH MORRISSEY
VEGAN RECIPES FROM THE ONE YOU LEFT BEHIND

Illustrations are © Automne Zingg, 2012, 2016
Recipes are © Joshua Ploeg, 2016
This edition is © Microcosm Publishing, 2016
Cover design by Meggyn Pomerleau
Book design by Joe Biel

First Printing, October 11, 2016

For a catalog, write:
Microcosm Publishing
2752 N. Williams Ave
Portland, OR 97227
or visit MicrocosmPublishing.com

ISBN 978-1-62106-203-5
This is Microcosm #255

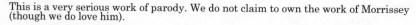

This is a very serious work of parody. We do not claim to own the work of Morrissey (though we do love him).

Distributed worldwide by Legato / Perseus and in the UK by Turnaround
This book was printed on post-consumer paper
Global labor conditions are bad, and our roots in industrial Cleveland in the 70s and 80s made us appreciate the need to treat workers right. Therefore, our books are
MADE IN THE USA

Library of Congress Cataloging-in-Publication Data

Names: Zingg, Automne. | Ploeg, Joshua.
Title: Defensive Eating with Morrissey : Vegan Recipes from the One You Left
    Behind / Automne Zingg ; recipes by Joshua Ploeg.
Description: Portland, OR : Microcosm Publishing, 2016.
Identifiers: LCCN 2016000081 | ISBN 9781621062035 (trade)
Subjects: LCSH: Vegan cooking--Recipes. | LCGFT: Cookbooks.
Classification: LCC TX837 .Z5534 2016 | DDC 641.5/636--dc23
LC record available at http://lccn.loc.gov/2016000081

DEFENSIVE EATING WITH MORRISSEY

Vegan Recipes from the One You Left Behind

Automne Zingg
Recipes by Joshua Ploeg

Microcosm Publishing
Portland, OR

FRIDGE

CONTENTS

In 2013, I was broke, living in Los Angeles, and going through a terrible breakup. It was probably one of the darkest times in my life and I felt inconsolable. I wasn't working. I wasn't eating. I wasn't drinking. I wasn't doing much of anything except writing depressing songs and listening to even more depressing ones from my youth. I found it curious that the bands that got me through the general malaise of being a sad teenage goth served as a type of sonic comfort food for me as an even sadder adult. Was I having a mid-life crisis?

The only thing that brought me comfort during that nightmare was drawing. I started to doodle images of Nick Cave crying over pints of ice cream, Siouxsie Sioux devouring tacos, and The Sisters Of Mercy stuffing their faces with Cinnabons. The more time passed, the more surreal these drawings became. Eventually, I started sharing them with others and everyone wanted to see Morrissey putting things in his mouth. Who wouldn't? I obliged and started doing a series of drawings of Morrissey hoarding food. Those drawings became a zine, and that zine is now a cookbook. Inspired by my illustrations, and playing on Morrissey's lyrics, Morrissey's influences, and some of the more absurd elements of pop culture, Joshua Ploeg has created some incredibly unique vegan recipes for anybody that believes meat is murder.

Defensive Eating with Morrissey: Vegan Recipes from the One You Left Behind is intended for Morrissey lovers, haters, and anyone who appreciates veganism, Marcel Proust and Oscar Wilde as much as they enjoy Garfield, Judge Judy, and a good "deez nuts" joke.

Nom Nom Nom.

xoxo
Automne Zingg

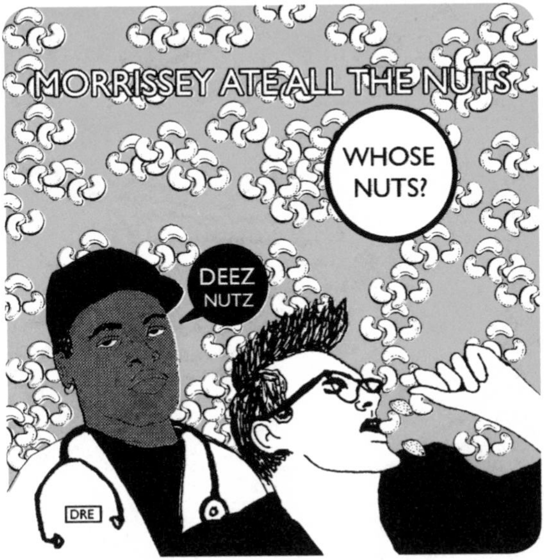
MORRISSEY ATE ALL THE NUTS
WHOSE NUTS?
DEEZ NUTZ
DRE

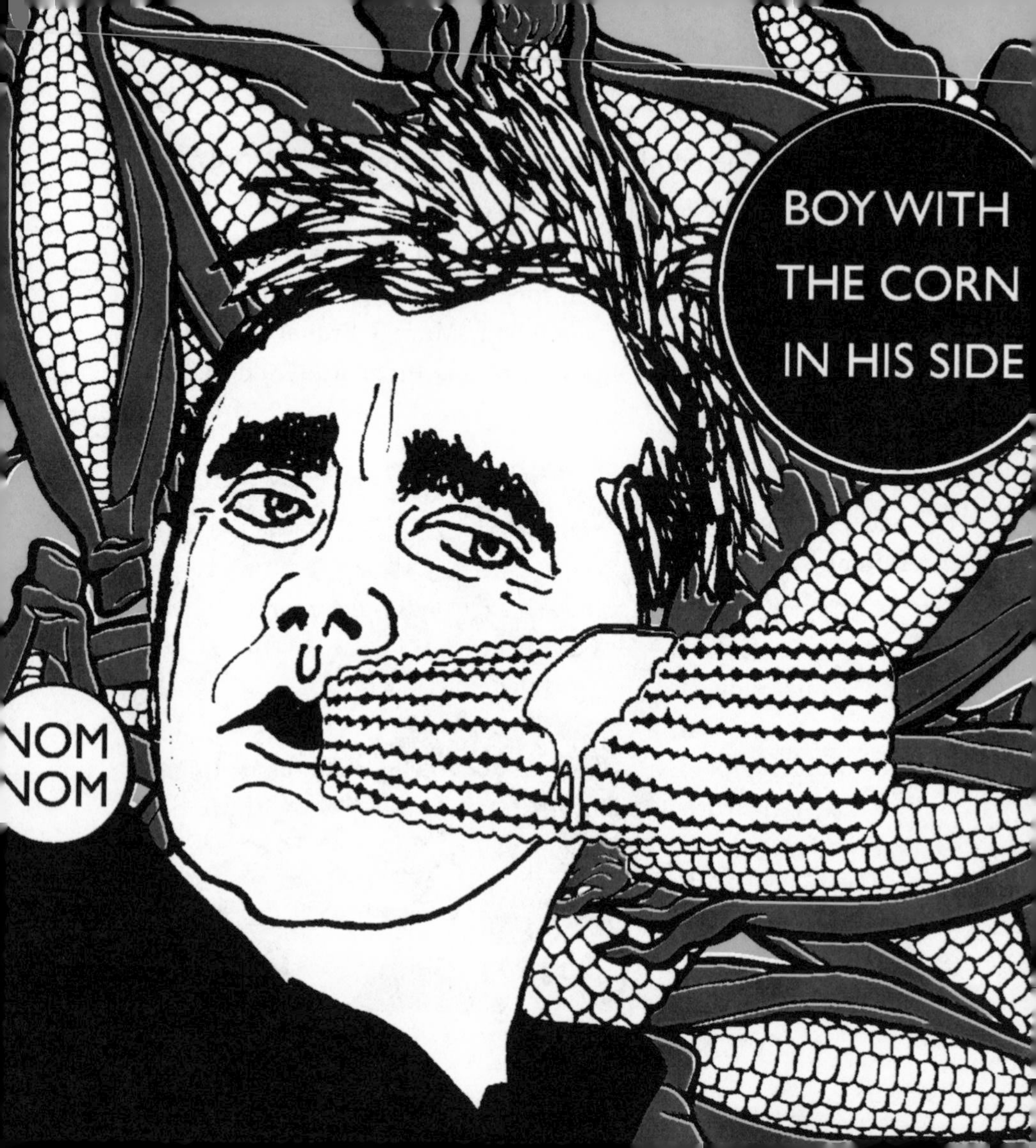
BOY WITH
THE CORN
IN HIS SIDE
NOM
NOM

CORN

6 ears corn

¼ cup coconut oil or margarine (or other oil)

1 teaspoon chili powder

1 teaspoon smoked paprika

½ teaspoon cumin

½ teaspoon ground coriander

¼ cup cornmeal

Salt and pepper, to taste

Shuck the corn cobs and set them in boiling water. Cover and turn off heat. Let stand for 10 minutes and then drain. Baste with melted margarine, roll in a combination of the other ingredients. Put in a baking pan under a broiler for 3 to 5 minutes per side, turning until broiled.

It's a quick recipe. Long ones make me feel so old inside (please die). Sprinkle with seasonings again, and serve with aioli or lime wedges.

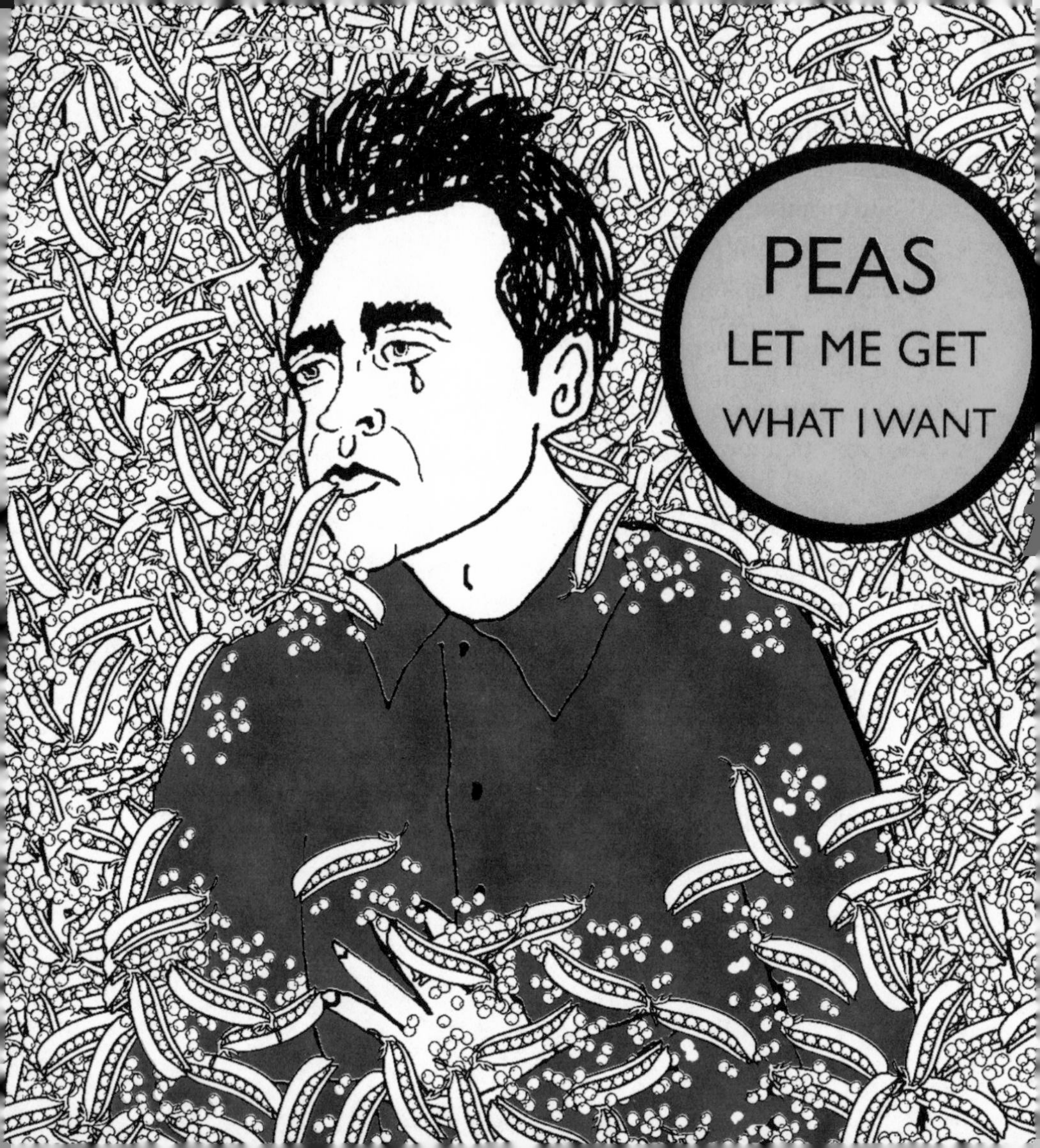
PEAS
LET ME GET
WHAT I WANT

PEAS

2 cups fresh peas, blanched and drained
12 garlic cloves (about one whole bulb), roasted
1 tablespoon olive oil
¼ cup fresh mint, chopped
¼ cup fresh Italian parsley, chopped
¼ teaspoon red pepper flakes
1 tablespoon lime juice
Salt and black pepper, to taste

Just so you know, you blanch peas by putting them in boiling water for about a minute, and then draining them.

You can roast garlic by cutting the end off the bulb, slathering it with a little oil and salt, and baking it in a small pan or oven-safe dish at 375 degrees for about 30 minutes. Cool and peel.

Okay! Now mix all ingredients together and season to taste.

Simple but great. You'll feel like you're being transported from this unhappy planet with all the carnivores and the destructors on it.

Balsamic vinegar is also nice in this, as well as some finely grated lime peel. Serve chilled. Works well with arugula or other tasty greens.

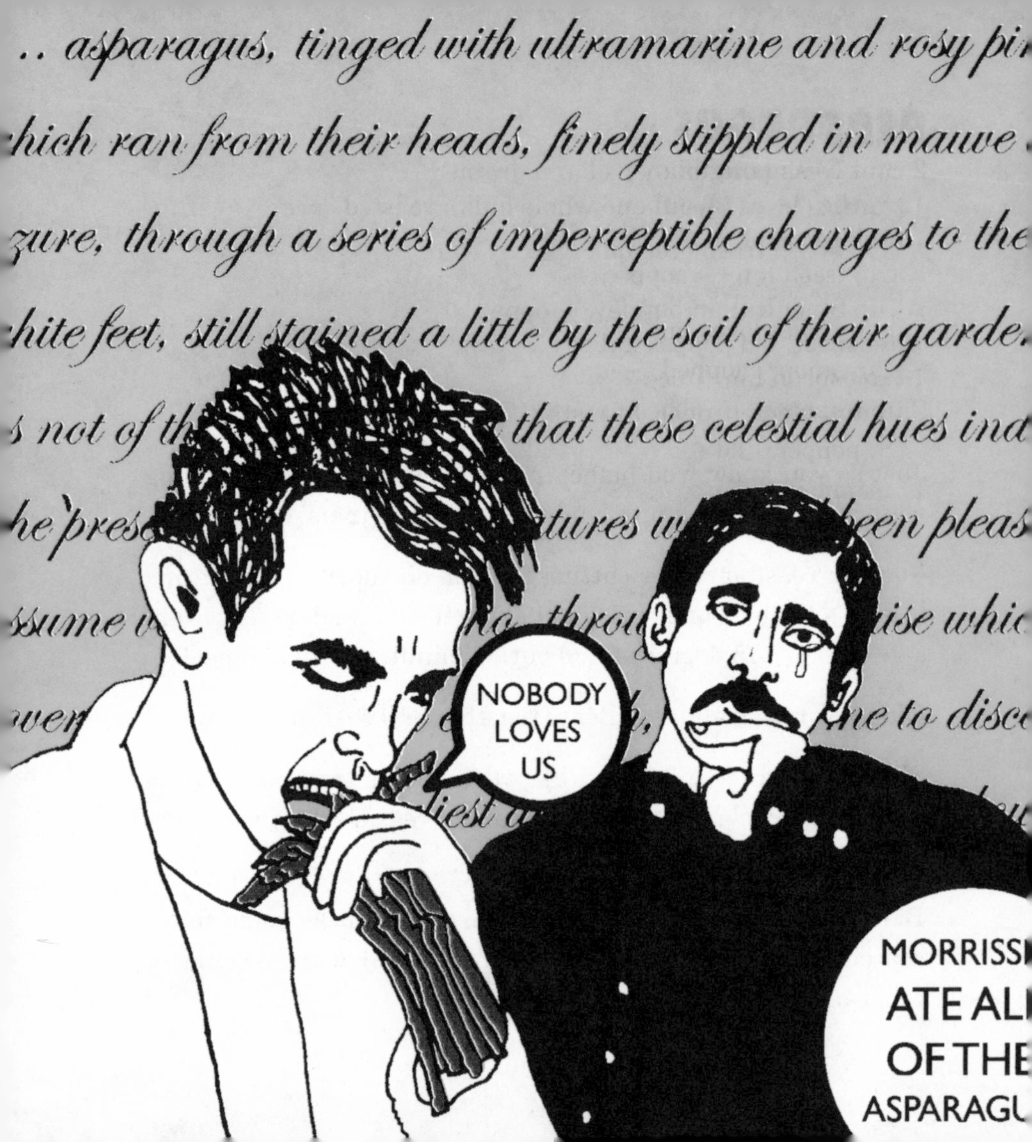
.. asparagus, tinged with ultramarine and rosy pi
hich ran from their heads, finely stippled in mauve
zure, through a series of imperceptible changes to the
hite feet, still stained a little by the soil of their garde
NOBODY LOVES US
MORRISS ATE AL OF THE ASPARAGU

ASPARAGUS

2 pounds asparagus

1 cup tomatoes, chopped

1 tablespoon fresh oregano, minced

1 tablespoon olive oil

2 to 3 garlic cloves, minced

¼ cup onion, chopped

2 tablespoons sun-dried tomatoes, pureed

Salt, pepper, and red pepper flakes, to taste

Balsamic vinegar to drizzle

Mix all ingredients together except balsamic vinegar, and then place in a casserole. Roast at 375 degrees for 20 minutes. Drizzle with balsamic vinegar, and then mix again.

You can cook it for less time, if desired.

But with a bit more time and a few more gentler words and looking back we will forgive.

Broil for 3 to 5 minutes to finish.

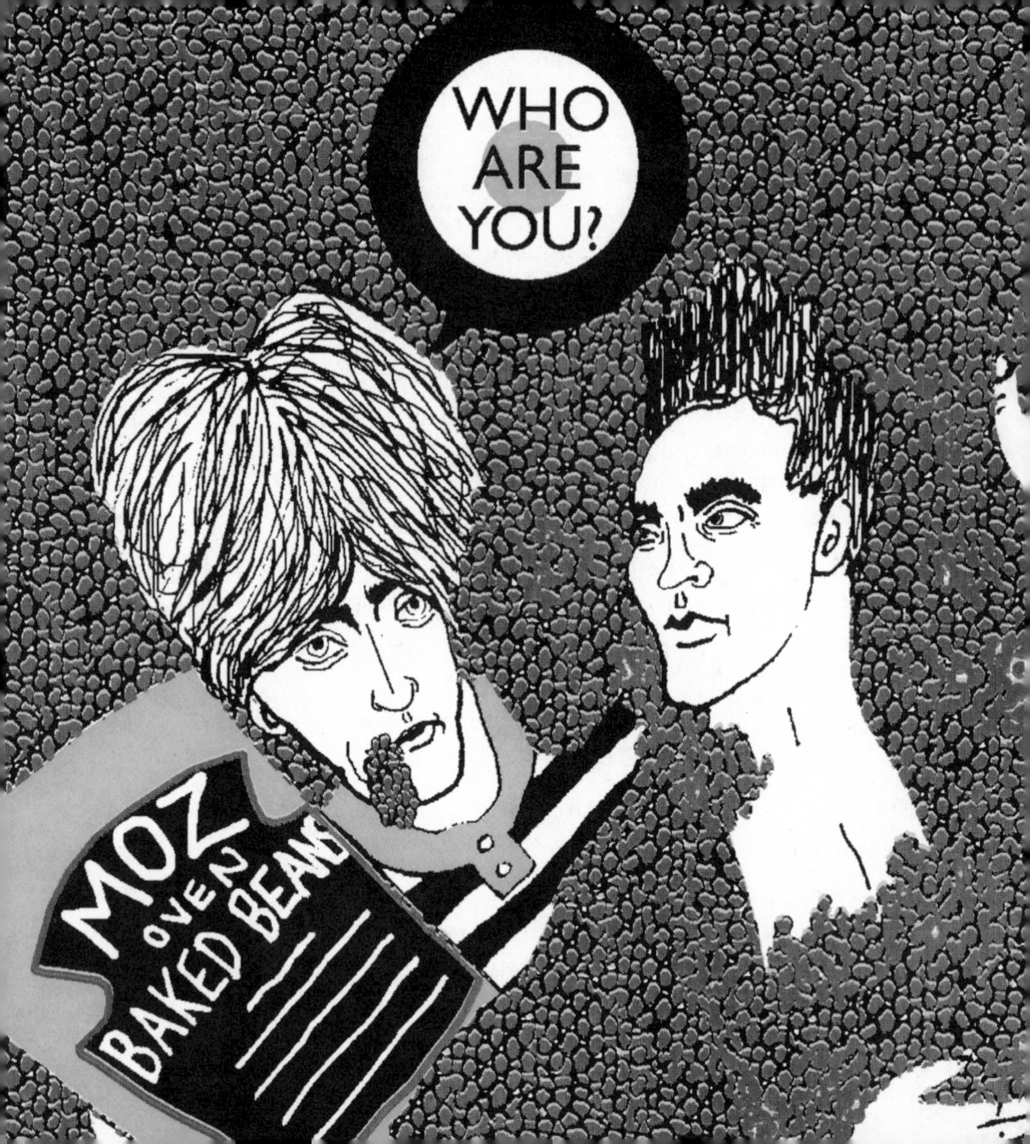
WHO ARE YOU?
MOZ OVEN BAKED BEANS

BEANS

2 cups dry beans (red, brown, or other suitable bean)
Bouquet garni (your choice of aromatic herbs)
1 onion, diced
2 garlic cloves, minced
1 cup crushed tomatoes
¼ cup tamarind puree or paste
Black pepper, to taste
½ teaspoon each cumin, coriander, and paprika
1 carrot, minced
2 tablespoons oil
2 tablespoons to ¼ cup brown sugar
Salt, to taste
A handful of mushrooms, sliced or chopped
HP sauce or vegan Worcestershire
2 scallions, minced (to garnish)

Submerge beans in water and soak overnight. Drain. Submerge in water again and bring to a boil. Lower to a simmer. Make sure beans are kept covered in water by adding more as needed. Add bouquet garni.

Add onion, garlic, tomatoes, tamarind paste, and black pepper. Cook for an hour, keeping water up. Add cumin, coriander, paprika and any other spices you wish. Add carrots, oil, and brown sugar. When beans are soft enough, add salt and mushrooms. At this point, it's okay to let the liquid cook off and the mixture thicken up a bit. (You can thicken it up even more with tomato paste, a little bit of starch, or something else if you'd like.)

Remove bouquet garni (it's just passing through this world on its way to somewhere civilized). Mash the beans a bit, if you like. Serve with toast, of course. Sprinkle with HP sauce or vegan Worcestershire and scallions.

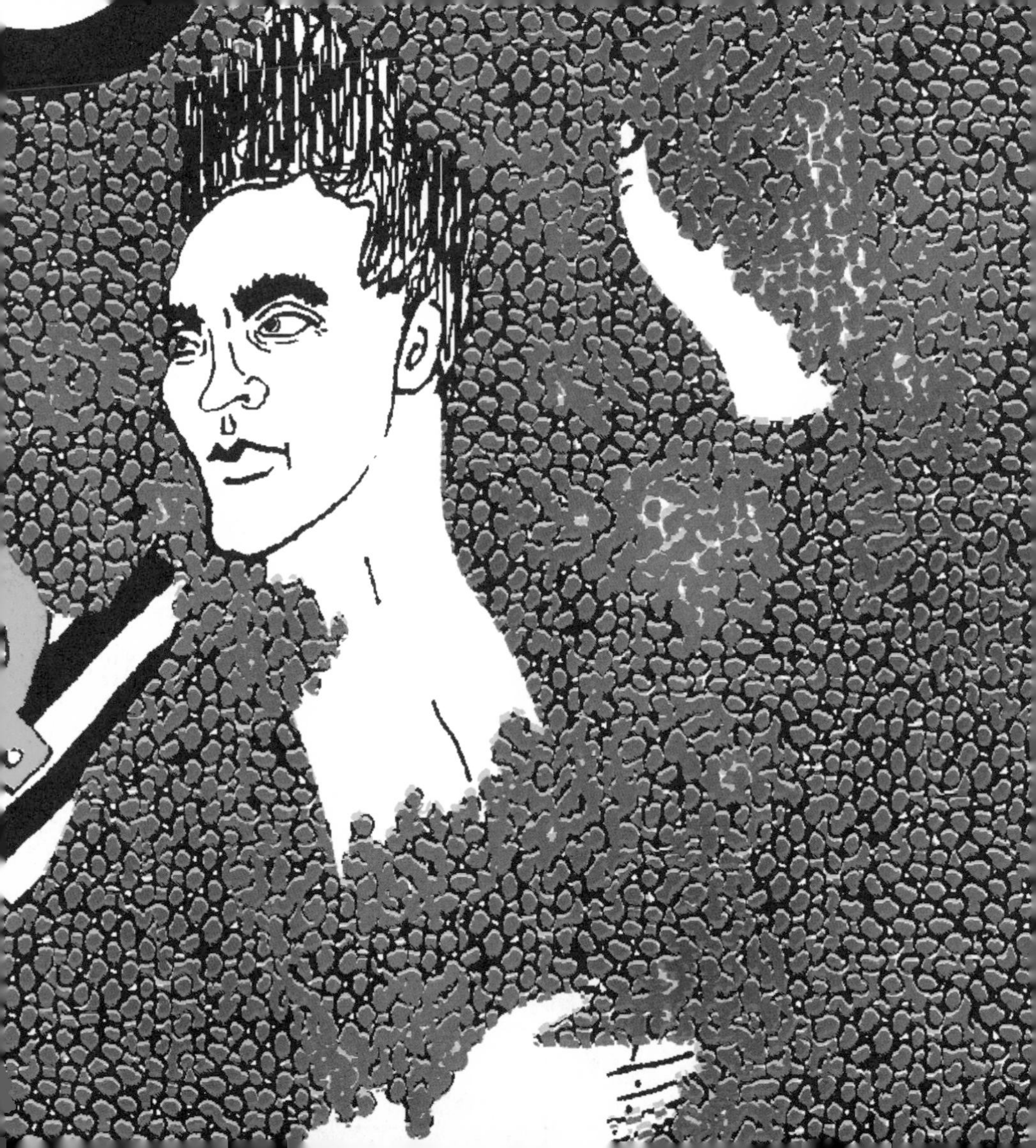

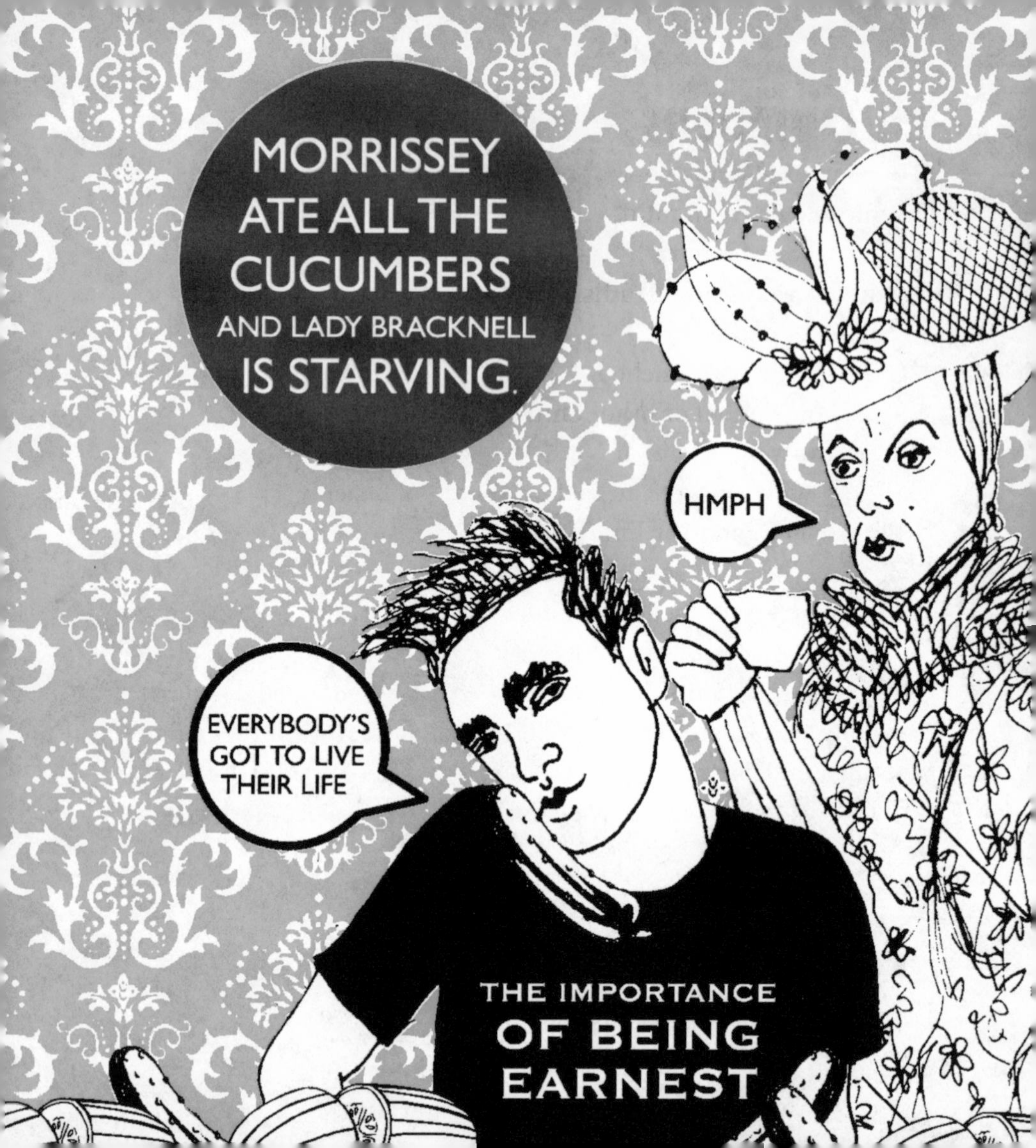
MORRISSEY
ATE ALL THE
CUCUMBERS
AND LADY BRACKNELL
IS STARVING.
HMPH
EVERYBODY'S
GOT TO LIVE
THEIR LIFE
THE IMPORTANCE
OF BEING
EARNEST

CUCUMBERS

3 cucumbers (stripe peeled, sliced, and cut into half moons)
2 tablespoons fresh mint, chopped
2 tablespoons fresh thai basil, chopped
½ cup daikon or other radish, diced
½ cup jicama, diced
½ cup edamame, blanched
1 teaspoon sambal or other chili paste (more to taste)
¼ cup thinly sliced onion
Salt and white pepper, to taste
1 tablespoon lemon or lime juice (or rice vinegar)
1 teaspoon toasted sesame oil
1 teaspoon sesame seeds, toasted

Mix all ingredients together except toasted seeds. Adjust seasonings to taste. In the past I have really tarted this salad up, but I'm determined not to make the same mistake this time around. Garnish with toasted sesame seeds, more herbs, and more chili paste.

Can be mixed in to a mizuna salad, or add seaweed for a nice combo.

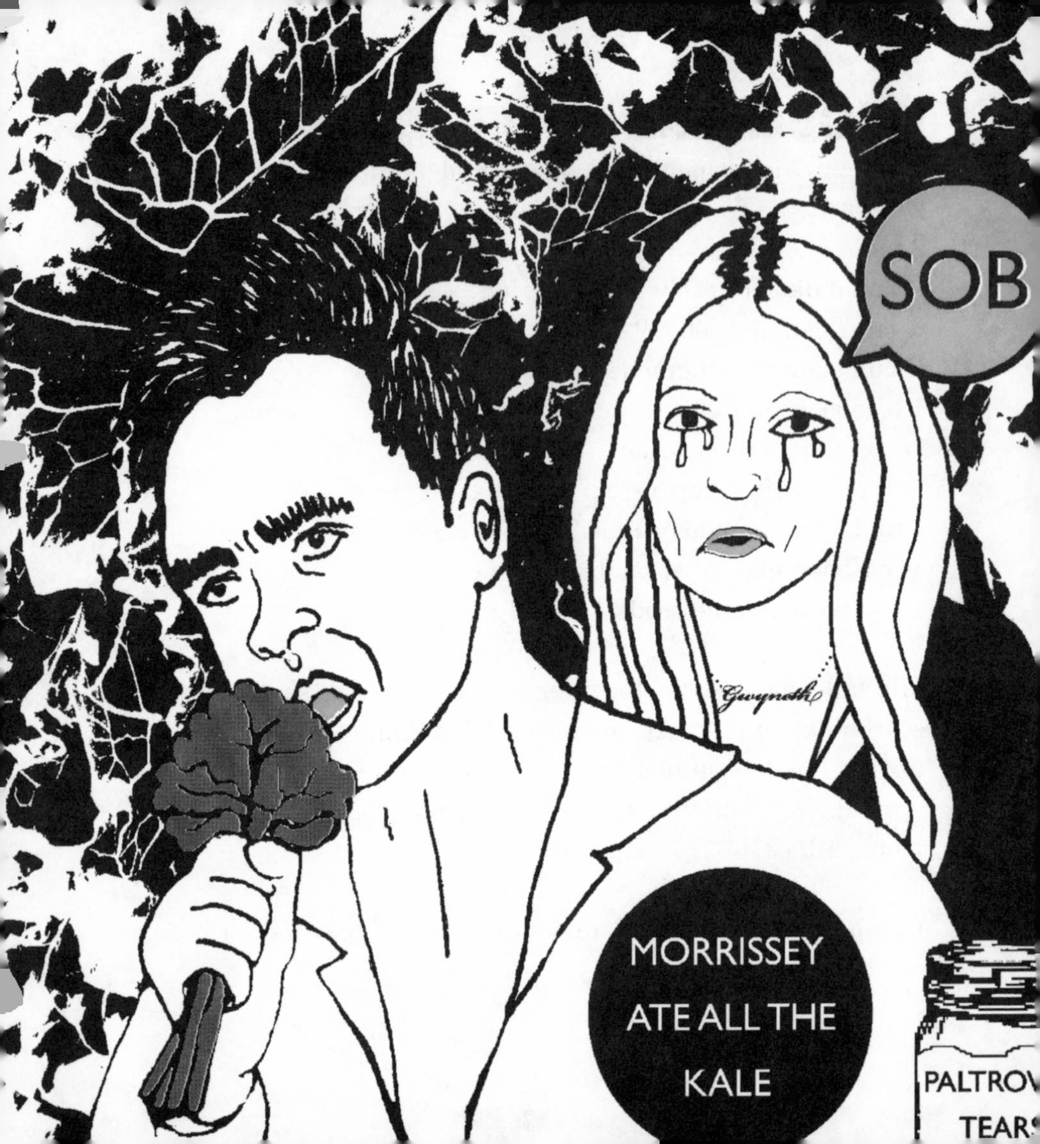
SOB
Gwyneth
MORRISSEY ATE ALL THE KALE
PALTROV
TEARS

SPICY KALE & SWEET POTATOES

2 or 3 spicy chilies and 2 poblano peppers

Salt and pepper, to taste

1 tablespoon lime juice (more to taste)

¼ to ½ teaspoon each paprika, chili power, cumin, and coriander

2 cups sweet potato, diced

2 heads of kale, chopped

2 garlic cloves, minced

¼ cup red onion, sliced or diced

1 onion, cut into thin strips

2 mangoes, peeled and diced

A couple tablespoons olive oil

Of course you can add chili paste or more peppers, if you like

Roast peppers at 400 degrees for 25 to 30 minutes. Let cool, seed, and cut into strips. Season with salt and lime juice, and then set aside. Cook sweet potatoes in olive oil with salt, pepper, and paprika until browned and crispy (doesn't really matter whether on stove top or oven).

Separately, cook greens with onion, garlic, lime juice, red onion, chili powder, cumin, coriander, and salt and pepper. Once greens wilt, add mango. Cook for a few more minutes. Toss in sweet potatoes and roasted chilies, and remove from heat. Make this as hot as you like (soil your britches hot). And no, I cannot steal a pair of jeans off a clothesline for you.

*This is bomb with coconut sour cream. Blend coconut cream (just the cream) with salt to taste and a couple tablespoons lemon juice, 2 tablespoons olive oil, 2 garlic cloves, and 1 wax pepper until smooth and creamy. Have it on the side with this dish and some chopped scallions. Good with black rice.

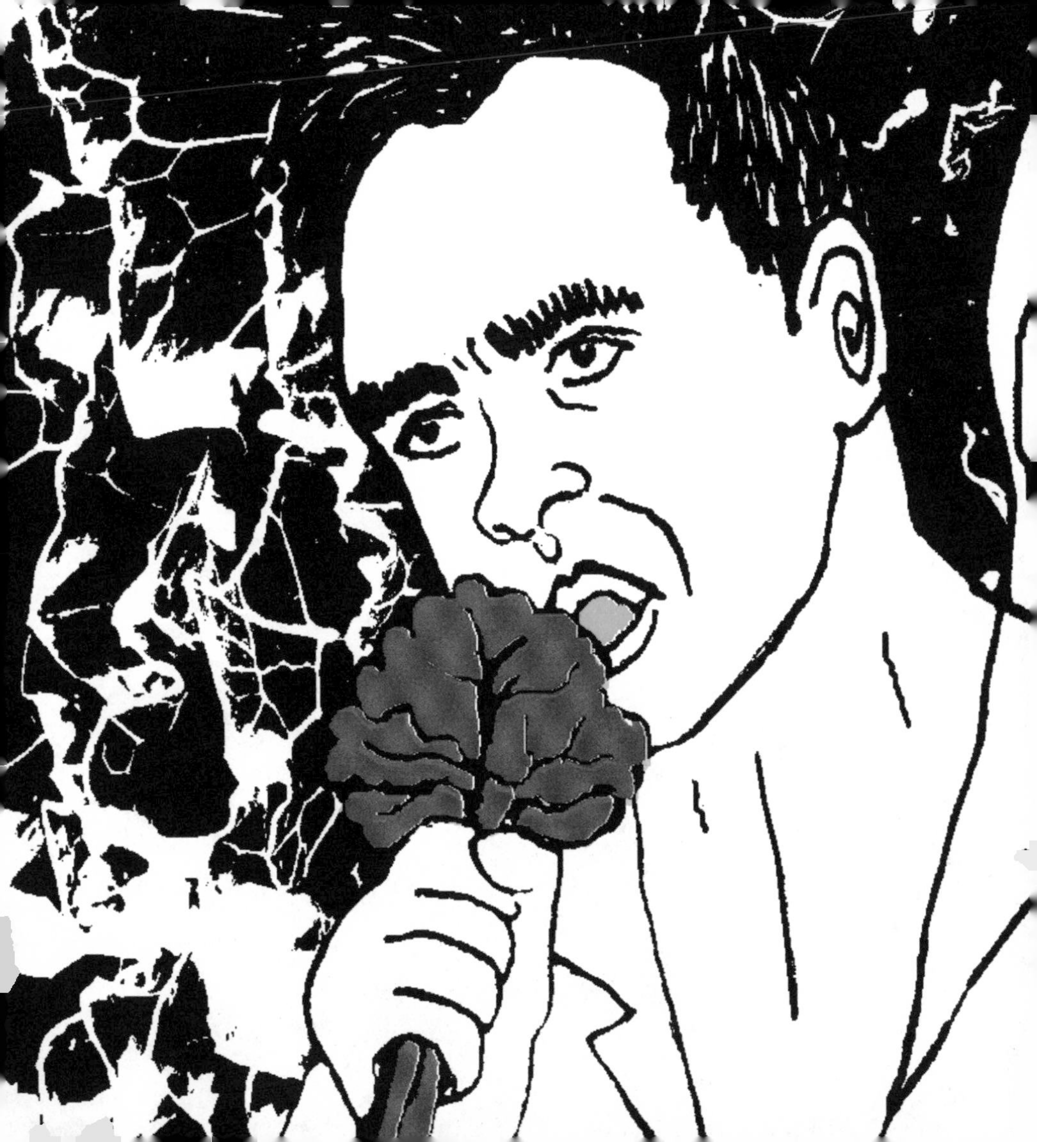

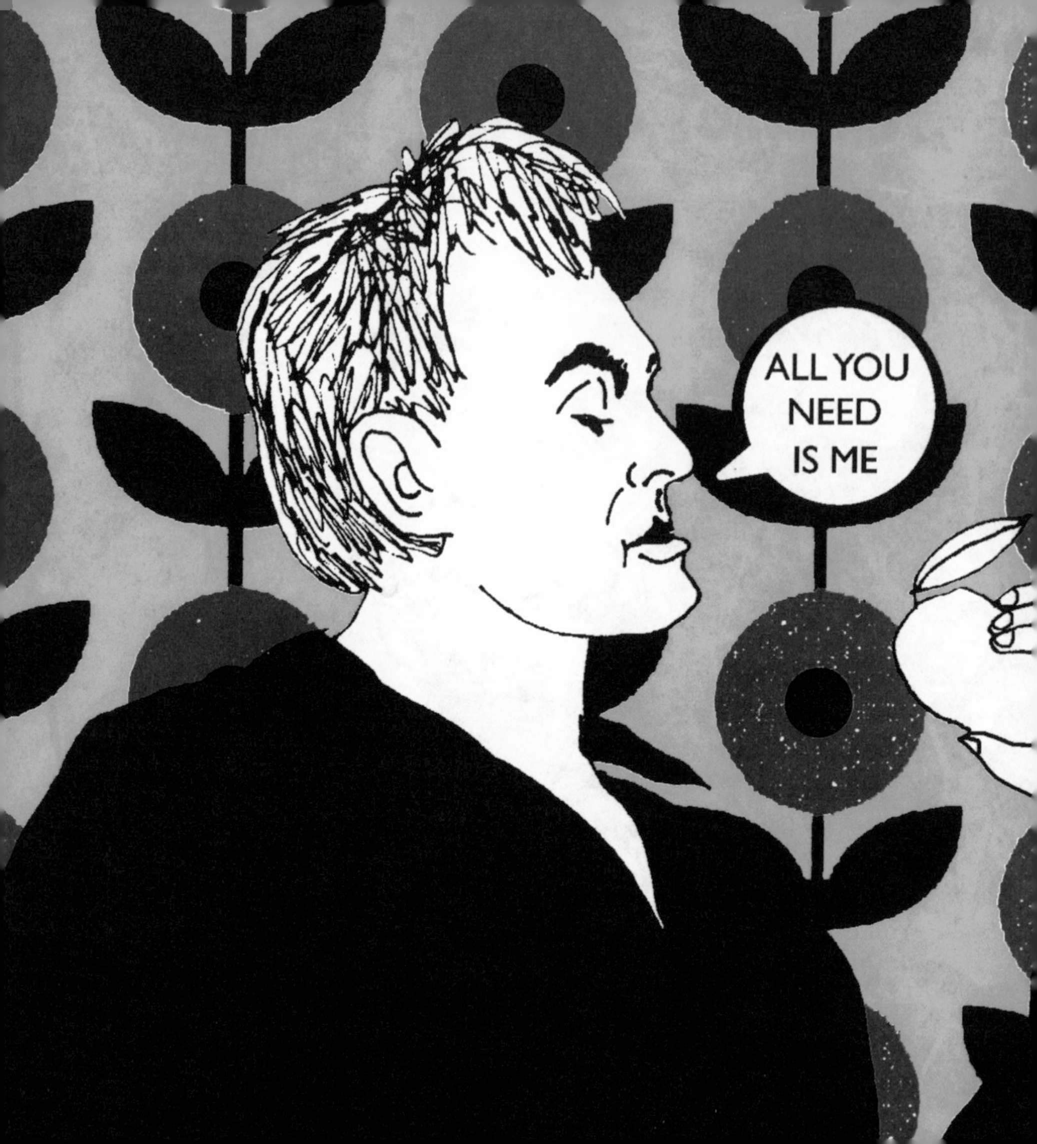
ALL YOU NEED IS ME

MANGO CHILI ICE CREAM

1 ½ cup vanilla soy creamer or coconut milk

1 ½ cup (or more) fresh or frozen mango

$^{1}/_{3}$ cup (or less) sugar or favorite sweetener

2 to 3 tablespoon lemon or lime juice

2 tablespoon mango vodka

½ teaspoon ginger

Salt, to taste

¼ teaspoon cayenne pepper (more to taste)

¼ teaspoon coriander

1 teaspoon chili powder or 1 to 2 fresh hot red chili

*Optionally you could use a spicy, flavorful red curry paste in this as well instead of chilies (couple of teaspoons or so)

Blend all ingredients until smooth. Use either an ice cream maker to get it done or do it yourself. Make it as dazzling or as spicy as you like. If you have the urge to eat it before it is fully ready, I'm sorry I have placed desire in you when there's nothing you can do with this desire.

You'll want to put it in the freezer and whisk it around every half hour until frozen.

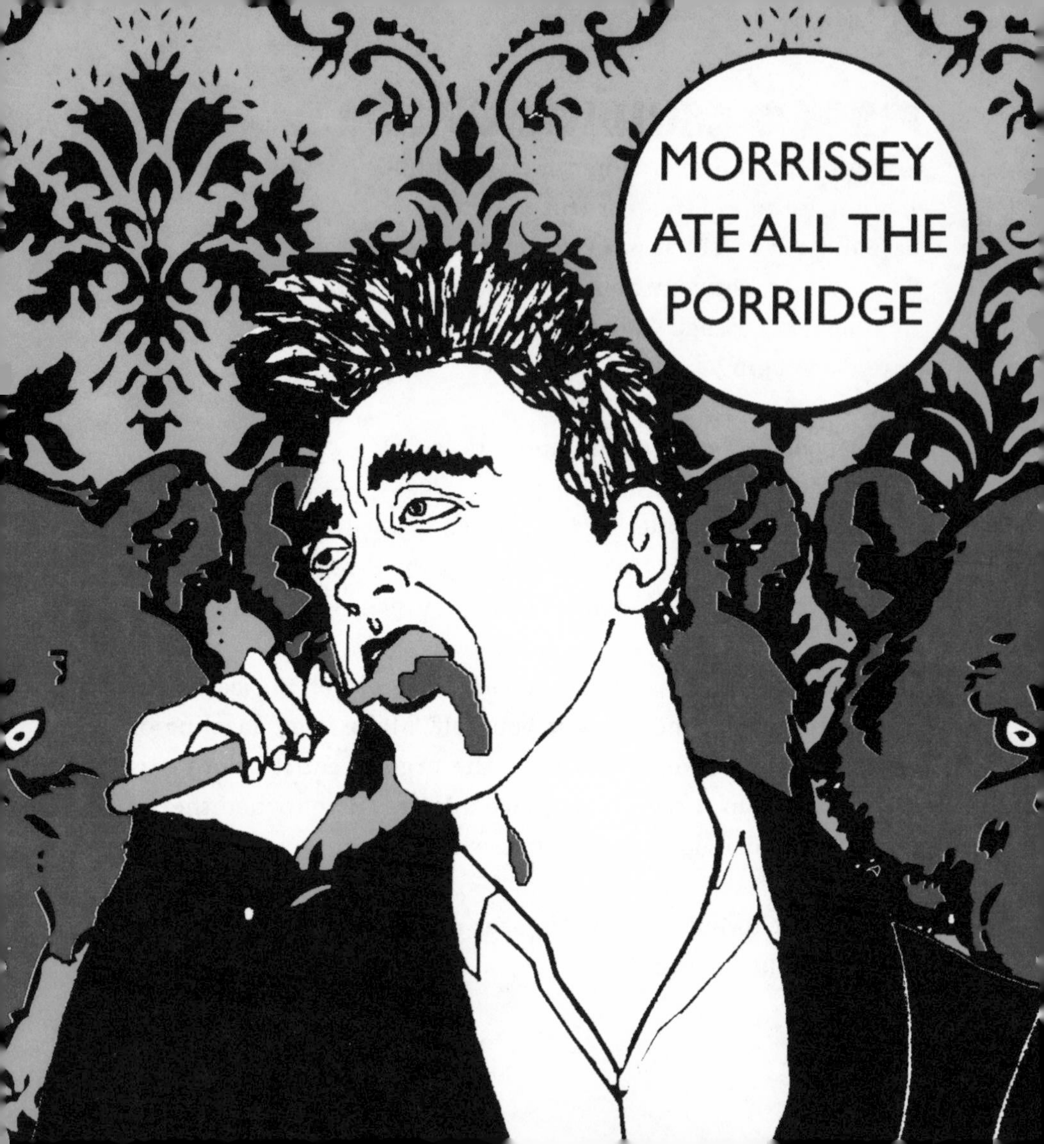
MORRISSEY
ATE ALL THE
PORRIDGE

PORRIDGE

1 cup coconut milk

2 cups broth

2 tablespoons oil or margarine

Salt and black pepper, to taste

½ cup onions, diced

½ cup pearl barley

½ cup Irish oats

1 tablespoon fresh parsley, minced

½ teaspoon each turmeric and coriander

Smoked paprika for sprinkling

Other things you could add on top: ribbons of sauteed red cabbage, shredded carrots, toasted cashews, golden raisins, sour kreem, lemon, fresh chopped onions and herbs, rosemary, caramelized curry apples, fried plantains, toasted unsweetened coconut, etc.

Porridge is highly underrated, more than you'll ever know. Much more fabulous than regular gruel, it has sustained many a pauper or trodden-upon sort of person over the centuries. I would say, "please sir, you'll want some more." But that joke isn't funny anymore.

Begin by sautéing onions in oil with a little salt and pepper in a heavy-bottomed pot. When onions turn translucent, add oats and broth. Simmer for 10 minutes with the lid on. Add barley, coconut milk, spices, salt and pepper and half or so of the parsley. Continue cooking for about 25 minutes or until grains are cooked, adding more liquid if necessary.

Serve in bowls with chosen additions, paprika, and parsley sprinkled on top.

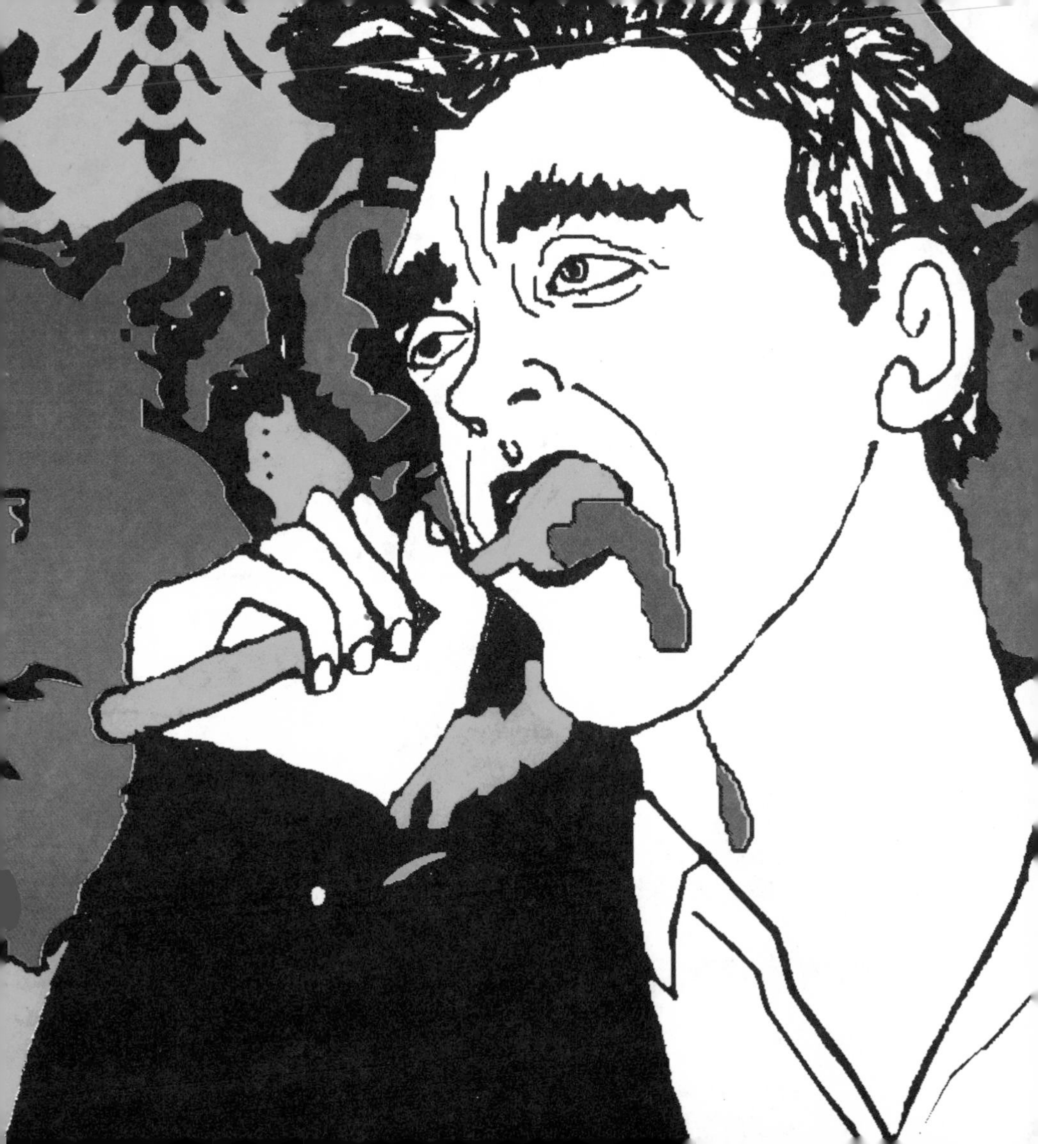

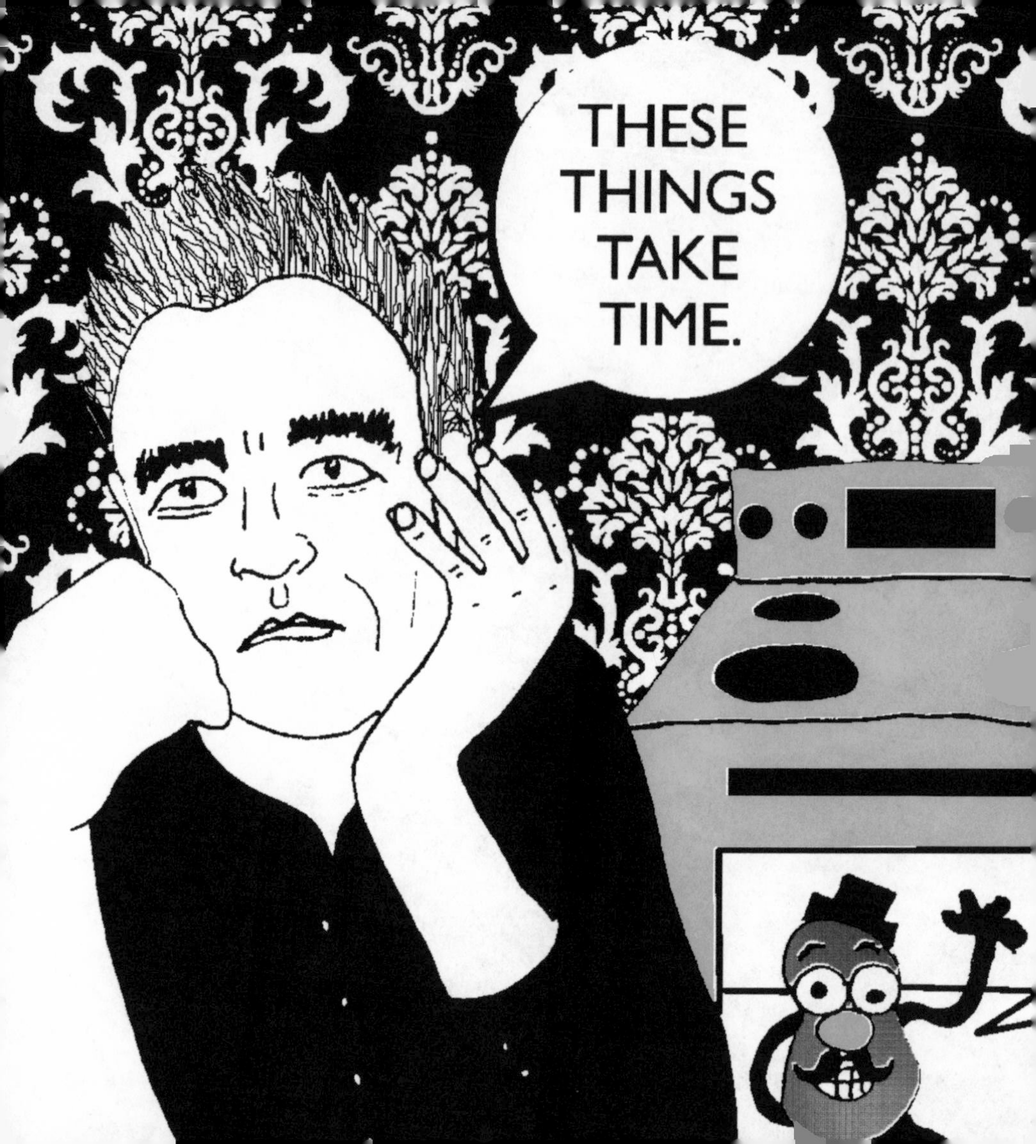
THESE THINGS TAKE TIME.

BAKED POTATO

4 large russet potatoes

1 cup white beans or silken tofu

2 tablespoons lemon juice or cider vinegar

¼ cup nutritional yeast

2 tablespoons chives, minced

Margarine or coconut oil for everything

2 cups black or pinto beans

½ cup chili sauce (tomato sauce with hot sauce in it works)

1 teaspoon each cumin, chili powder

A couple tablespoons tamari

½ cup reconstituted soy protein or chopped mushrooms

2 tablespoons tomato paste

1 cup onions, diced

2 garlic cloves, minced

½ cup green bell pepper, chopped

A little white pepper

Some oil for sauté and blending

1 teaspoon prepared mustard

Prick potatoes with a fork and wrap in foil. Bake at 375 degrees for an hour. Check to make sure they are done.

While that is happening, sauté half of the onions, garlic, bell pepper and soy protein in a little oil, adding tamari. Cook until browned. Add beans, tomato paste, chili sauce, cumin, and chili powder. Cook for 10 minutes, adding more liquid if needed while adjusting seasonings. Lower heat to warm when ready. Basically, this is just a quick chili topping.

Blend tofu or white beans with a couple tablespoons of oil, salt and white pepper to taste, lemon juice, and mustard. Put in fridge.

Add all of your fixins to split potato until repressed, but remarkably dressed. Slather with margarine or coconut oil, then add chili, nooch, sour kreem, diced onion. Sprinkle with chives. You can mix in the nutritional yeast with a favorite seasoning blend to jazz it up. Of course, some vegan cheez or bacon bits can be thrown on to send it O-T-T.

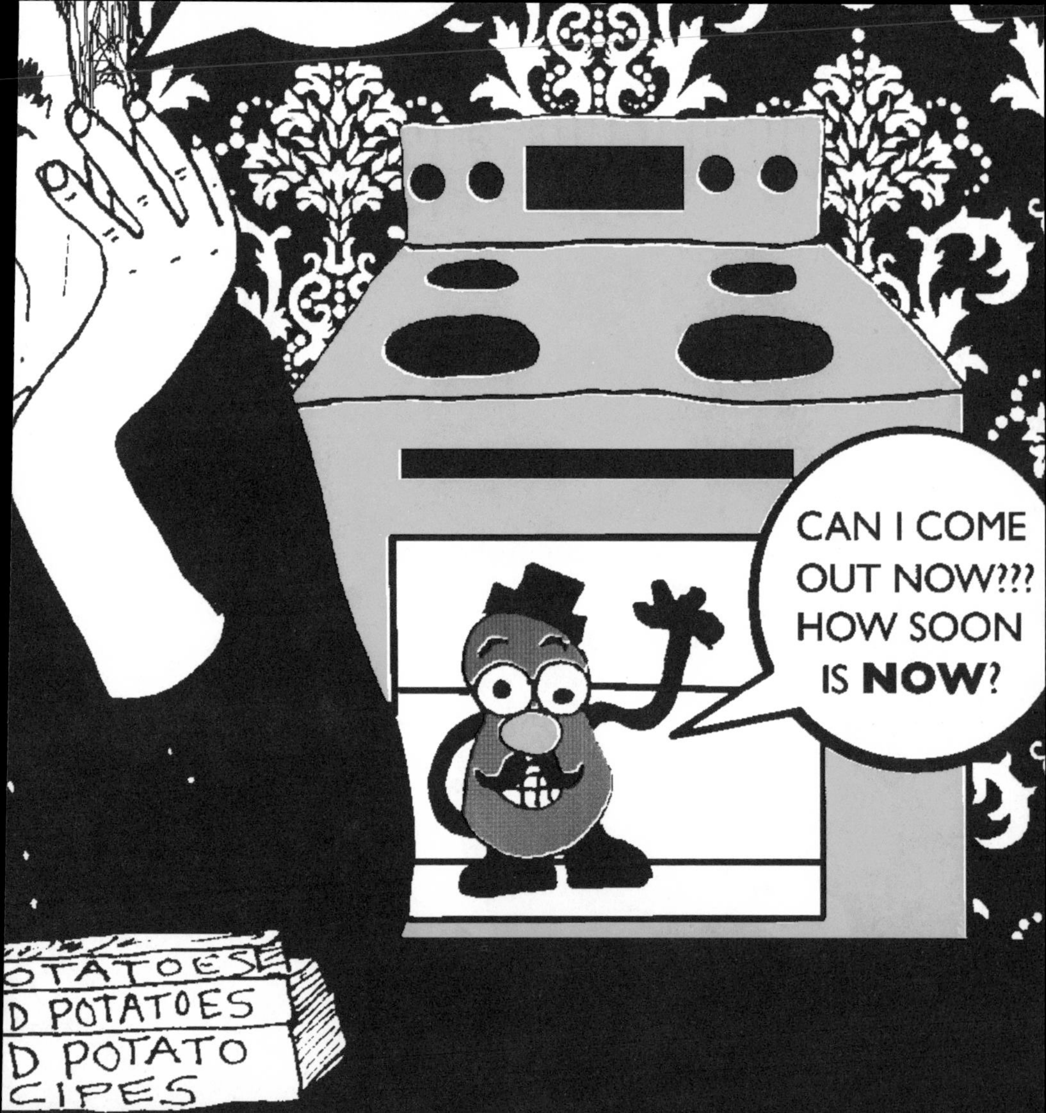
CAN I COME OUT NOW??? HOW SOON IS **NOW**?
OTATOES
D POTATOES
D POTATO
CIPES

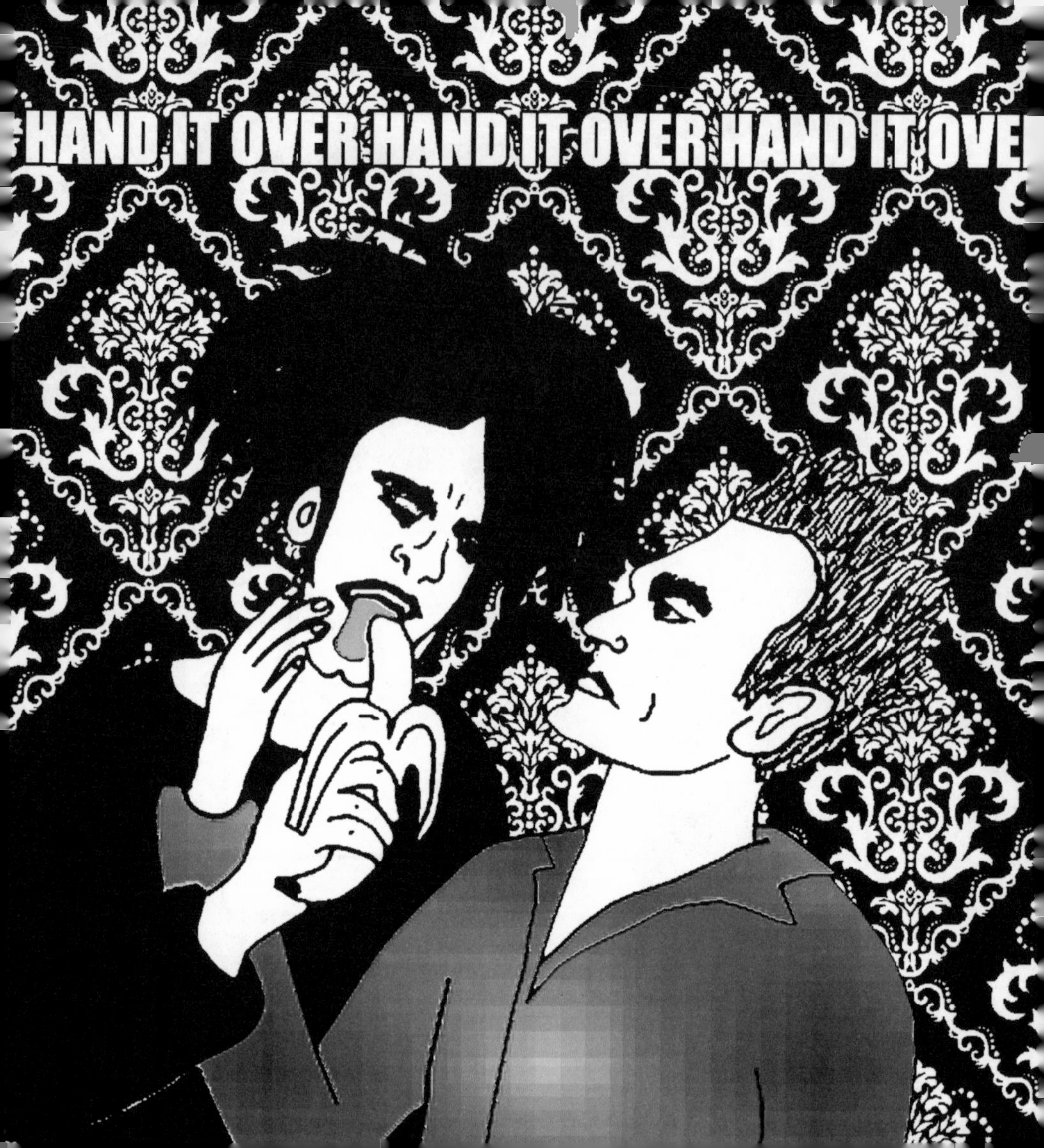
HAND IT OVER HAND IT OVER HAND IT OVE

BANANAS

4 bananas
1 teaspoon ginger, minced
4 large spring roll wrappers
2 tablespoons cinnamon
Sprinkle of lime juice
4 lime wedges
A few tablespoons of sugar
½ teaspoon vanilla
1 teaspoon turmeric
A little salt
Oil for frying

You'll want to mix the cinnamon and sugar together for this.

Coat bananas with a little lime juice, half of the cinnamon sugar, ginger, vanilla, turmeric, and salt. Roll up nicely in those spring roll wrappers, good n tight. You do not want liquid seeping out. It might getcha!

Place them carefully in hot oil (around 375 degrees). Don't be afraid. This beautiful creature must die! Fry in the oil, turning once, until nicely browned. Keep an eye on these bananas you so fancifully fry to make sure they don't burn.

Drain on absorbent paper. Dust with cinnamon sugar and serve with lime, and some nice ginger syrup and jam.

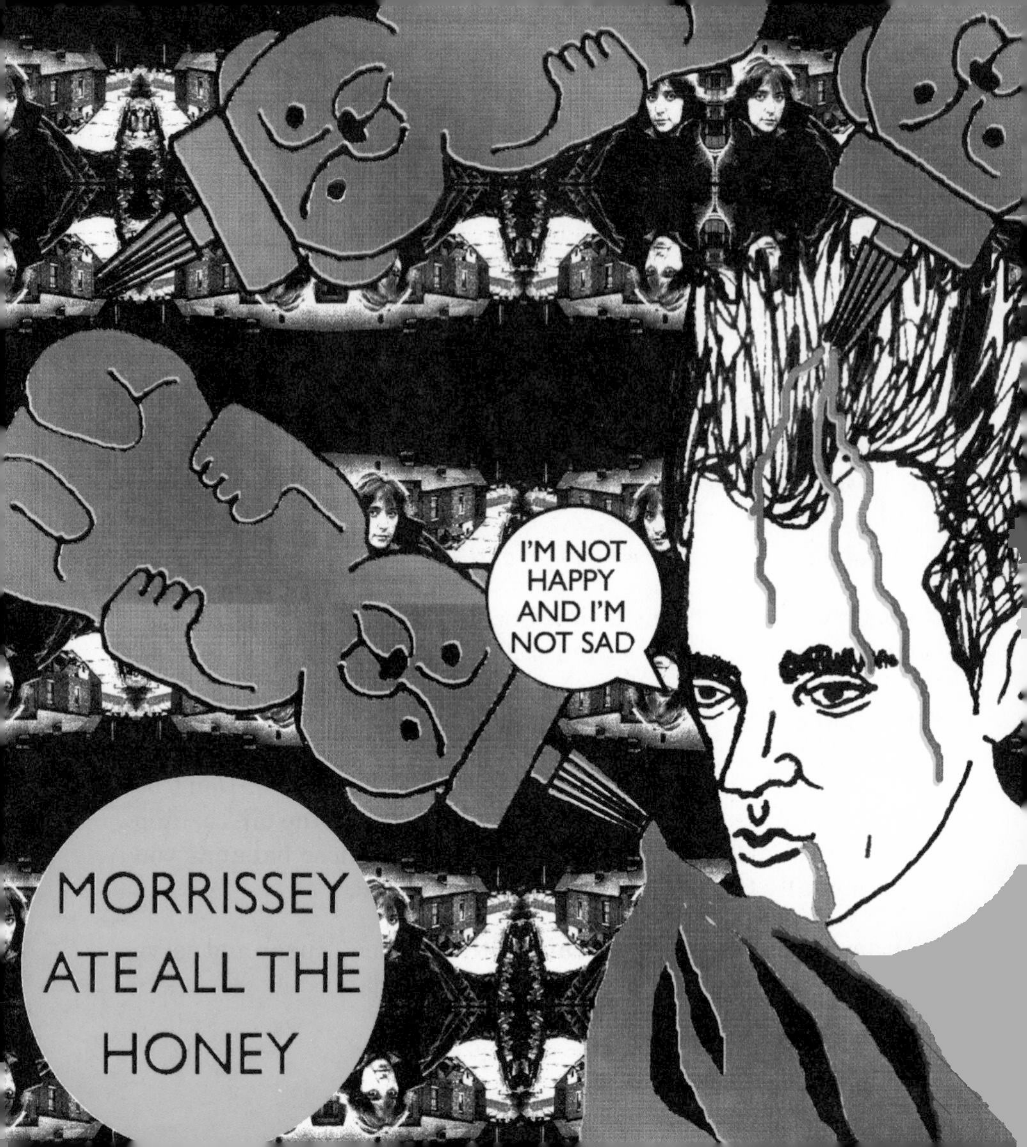
I'M NOT HAPPY AND I'M NOT SAD
MORRISSEY ATE ALL THE HONEY

HONEY

½ cup agave

½ teaspoon lavender essence

Salt, as needed

Phyllo dough (1 package will certainly be enough)

1 cup margarine or coconut oil

1 cup sugar

2 cups pistachios, walnuts, or other, finely chopped (have a little extra on hand to sprinkle)

½ teaspoon rosewater

½ teaspoon each cardamom, cinnamon, allspice (mixed together)

Heat agave with lavender essence and a little salt while stirring. Set aside to cool.

Grease a 9 in x 13 in baking pan. Place a layer of phyllo down—you may have to tear extra sheets to cover the whole area properly. Be smart and use your head, although most people keep their brains between their legs, don't you find? Lightly oil the sheet. Place down another and oil. Repeat.

Follow with $\frac{1}{3}$ of the nuts, spices, and sugar. Drizzle with lavender agave. Repeat this whole thing again to make a second layer, but only two thick this time. And then once more. Complete with a final layer of phyllo two sheets thick on top. Oil the top, and then sprinkle with nuts, sugar, a little spice, and rosewater (lightly). A little salt may be sprinkled too at any point. If you are using a margarine-type of spread, it might be plenty salty without any additions.

Bake at 350 degrees until golden: about 35 to 45 minutes. Check on it though at the 25-minute mark just to see what is happening.

Cut and serve.

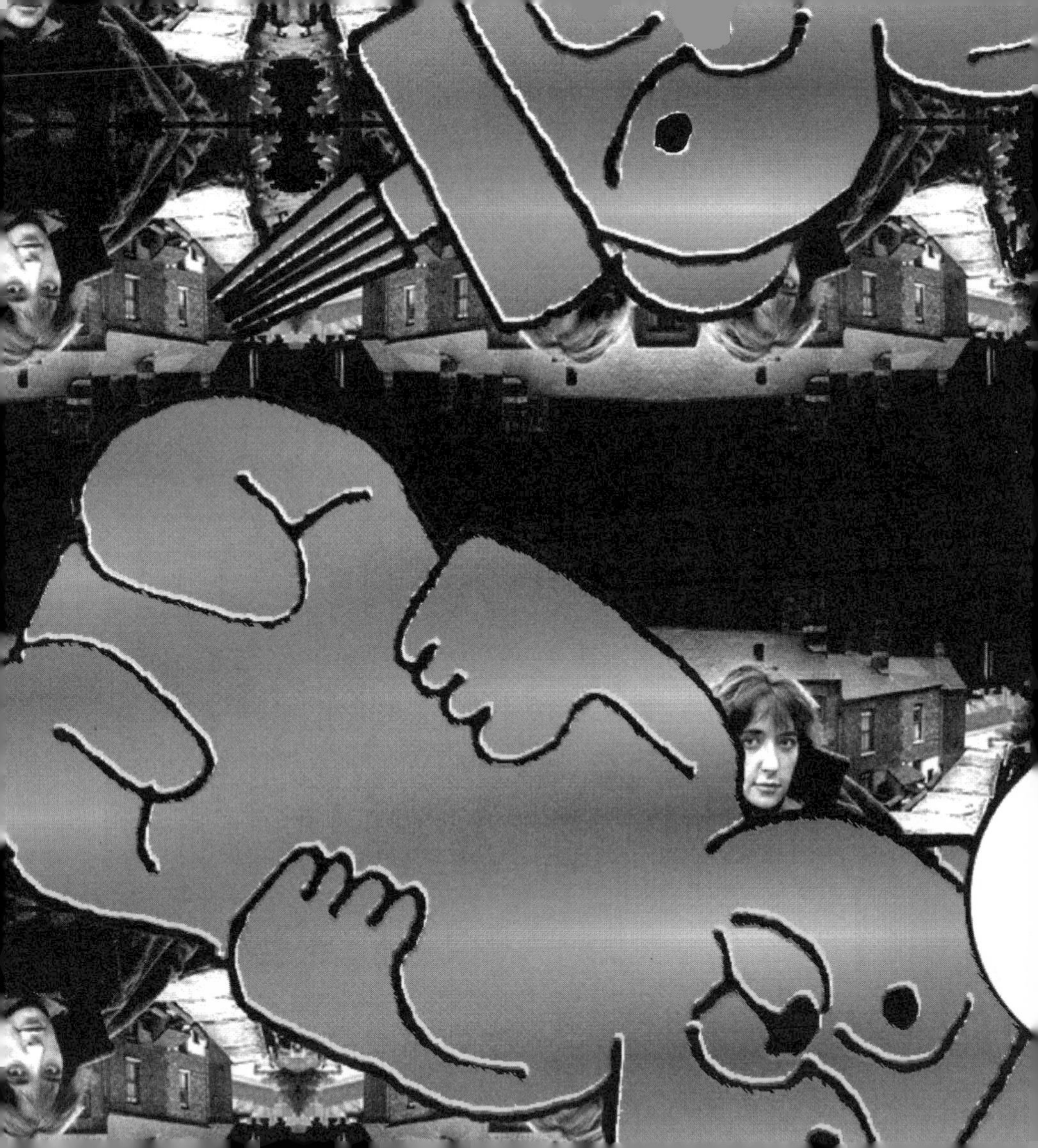

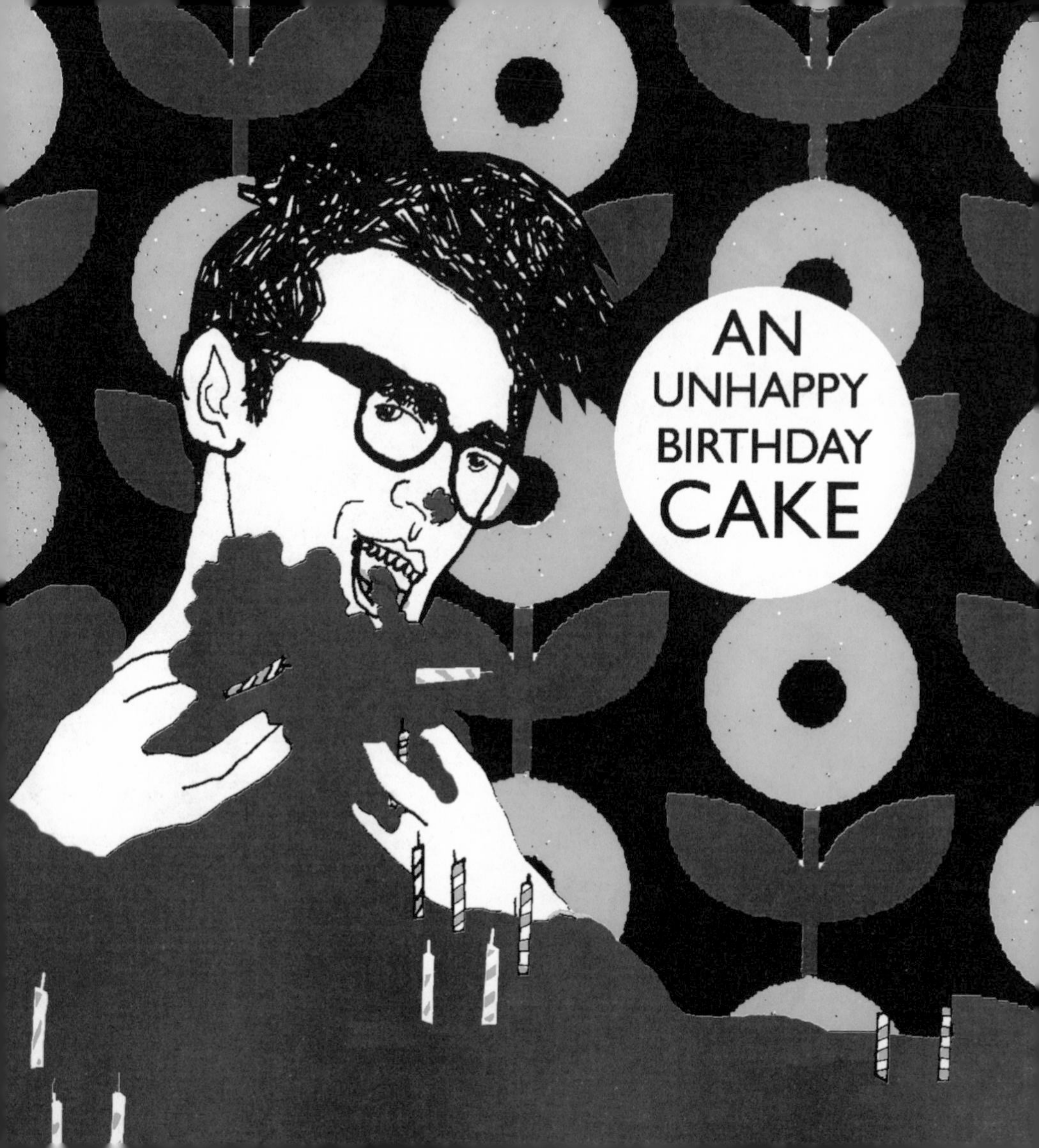
AN
UNHAPPY
BIRTHDAY
CAKE

CAKE

¼ cup sugar

½ cup oil

1 cup vegan sour cream or coconut milk with lemon juice

½ cup soy or other milk

2 ½ teaspoons lemon zest, grated

2 teaspoons orange zest, grated

$^1/_3$ cup lemon juice (some extra to make a glaze)

1 ½ cups zucchini, grated

2 ¼ cups flour

1 teaspoon baking powder

1 ½ teaspoons baking soda

½ teaspoon salt

Powdered sugar to make a glaze

You can add slivered almonds, walnuts, or whatever to this.

Mix all ingredients together except powdered sugar (dry ingredients first, then add the wet). Pour into a lightly greased, square cake pan (or rectangle; should be fairly large) and bake at 350 degrees for 40 minutes or until done.

If you have extra zucchini, cut it into ribbons and coat in some sugar for garnish. Grate more lemon peel and orange peel too. There's even more to do, but now you feel so ashamed because you've only got two hands.

Next, of course, mix powdered sugar and some extra lemon juice to make a glaze. I would put in a touch of salt. Proportions are up to you, depending on whether you want it to be more runny or not. For a frosting-like consistency, add margarine and a little vanilla, and use more powdered sugar and less liquid.

Cool the cake, then glaze or frost and decorate with some of the tasty ribbons of zucchini and lemon peel. You could half and half the zucchini with carrots.

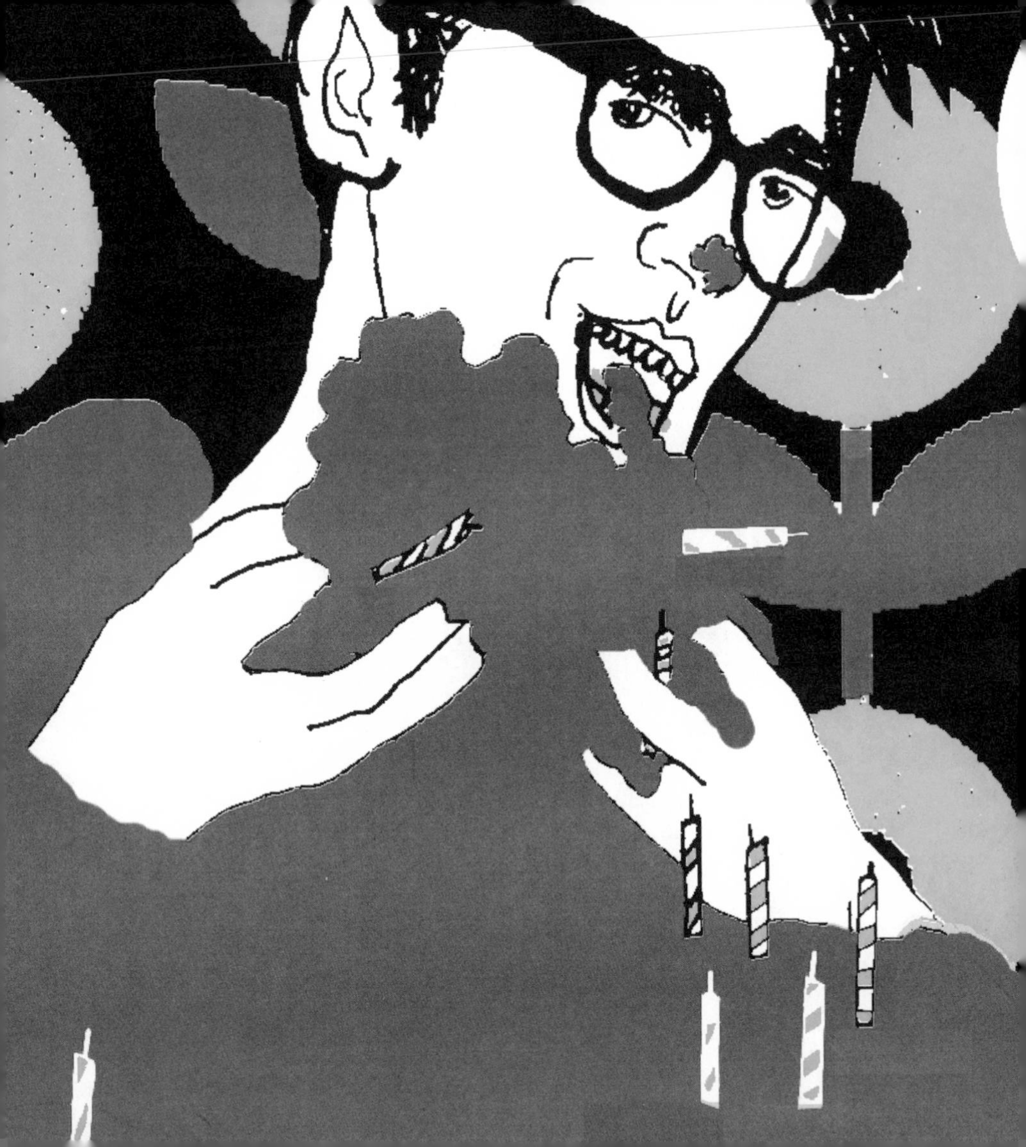

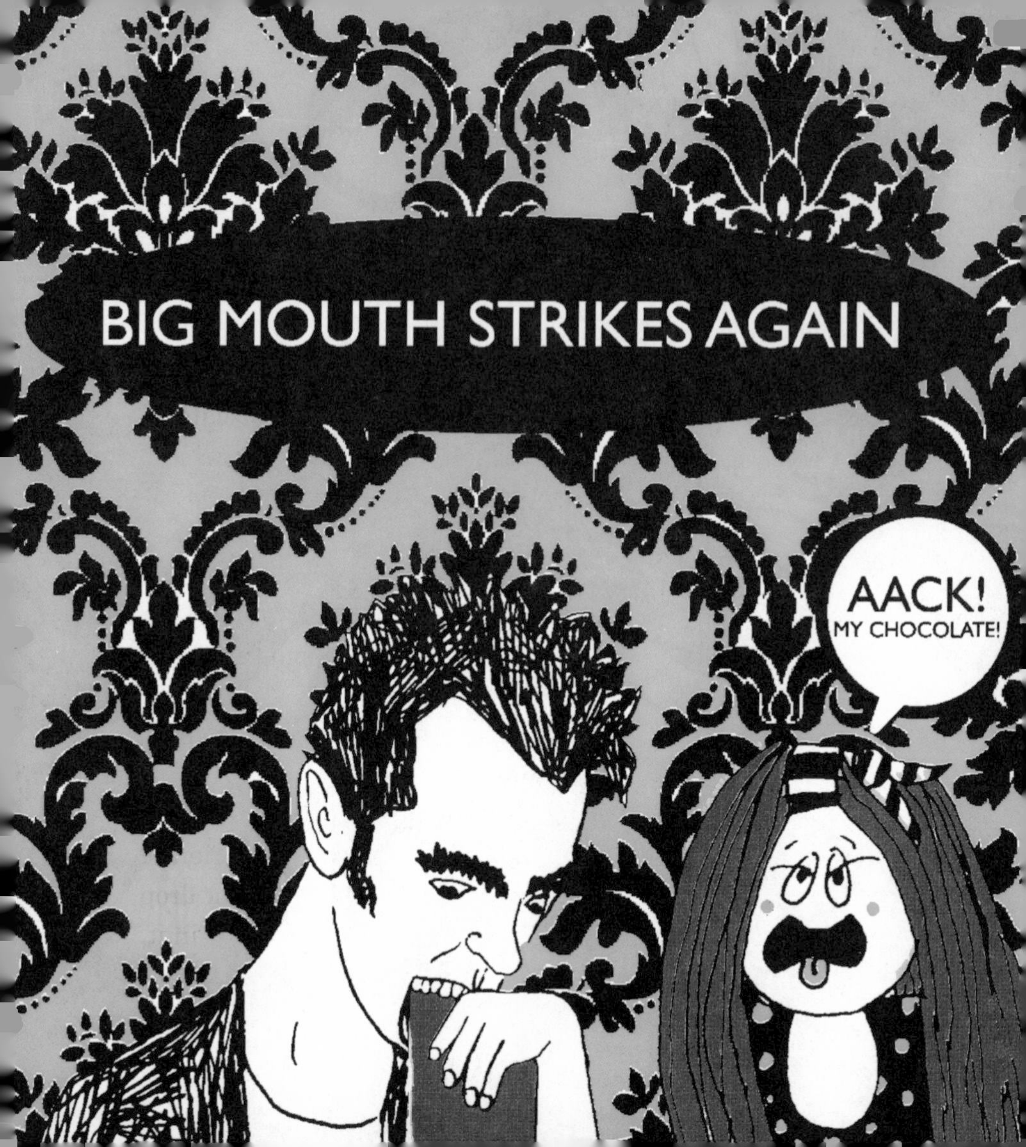
BIG MOUTH STRIKES AGAIN
AACK! MY CHOCOLATE!

CHOCOLATE

2 ounces bittersweet or dark chocolate, chopped
½ cup cocoa powder
A few tablespoons agave or maple syrup
4 cups soy, coconut, or other vanilla creamer
A pinch of salt

So you've been dreaming of a rich, decadent hot chocolate? I don't believe you. You don't dream about anyone except yourself. Well, now you can!

Melt chocolate in about a cup of the creamer in a good-size saucepan and stir. Add cocoa powder and whisk around—it should start to thicken. Add the rest of the ingredients and cook for a few minutes more. Cool a bit before serving. Drink most of it, and give the rest to a friend (god knows you've got yours).

You can sprinkle maple sugar, cocoa-cinnamon powder, smoked paprika, or vegan bacon salt on top for an interesting experience. Of course, add veg marshmallows or "whipped scream," or drop a salted caramel in there. The more cocoa powder you put in it, the thicker it will be.

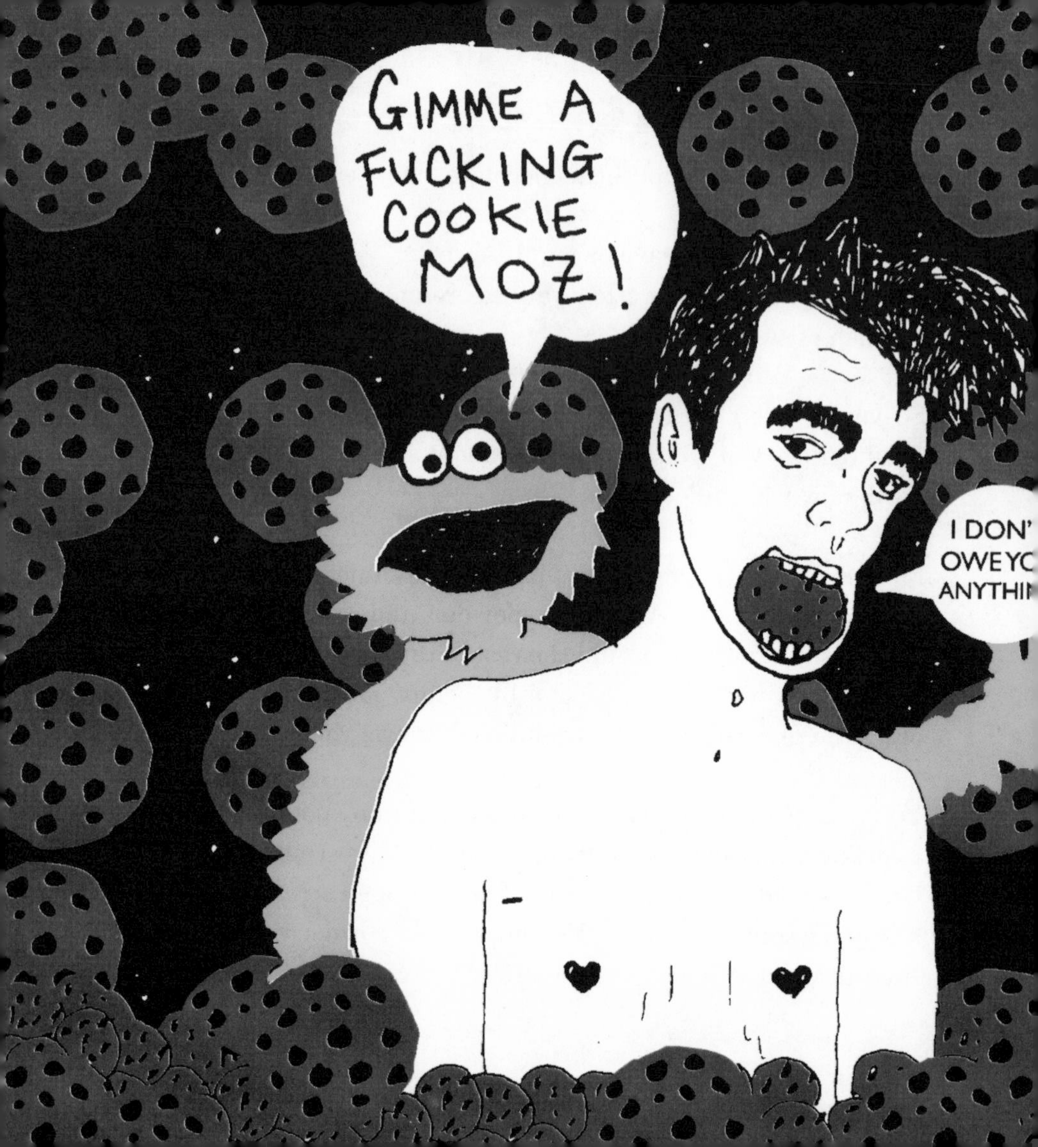
GIMME A FUCKING COOKIE MOZ!
I DON’
OWE YO
ANYTHI

COOKIES

½ cup sugar
½ cup brown sugar
$^2/_3$ cup almond butter
½ cup margarine, shortening, or coconut oil
1 $^1/_3$ cups flour
1 ½ teaspoons baking powder
Salt, to taste (use less if almond butter is salted)
½ cup almonds, chopped
1 teaspoon vanilla
½ teaspoon almond extract
2 tablespoons almond milk
24 whole almonds
Sugar, to sprinkle

Mix wet ingredients together. Add in the dry (except whole almonds).

Cover and refrigerate for a few hours. Shape dough into little balls and place them on a cookie sheet a few inches apart. Flatten balls with a fork. Place an almond in the center of each and sprinkle with sugar. Bake at 375 degrees for 10 to 12 minutes or until browned.

Cool on a wire rack before eating and don't lose faith (you know it's gonna happen someday). Of course, if you do lose faith just have some fun and eat them while still warm.

Morrissey's
HANDSOME DEVIL FOOD CAKE

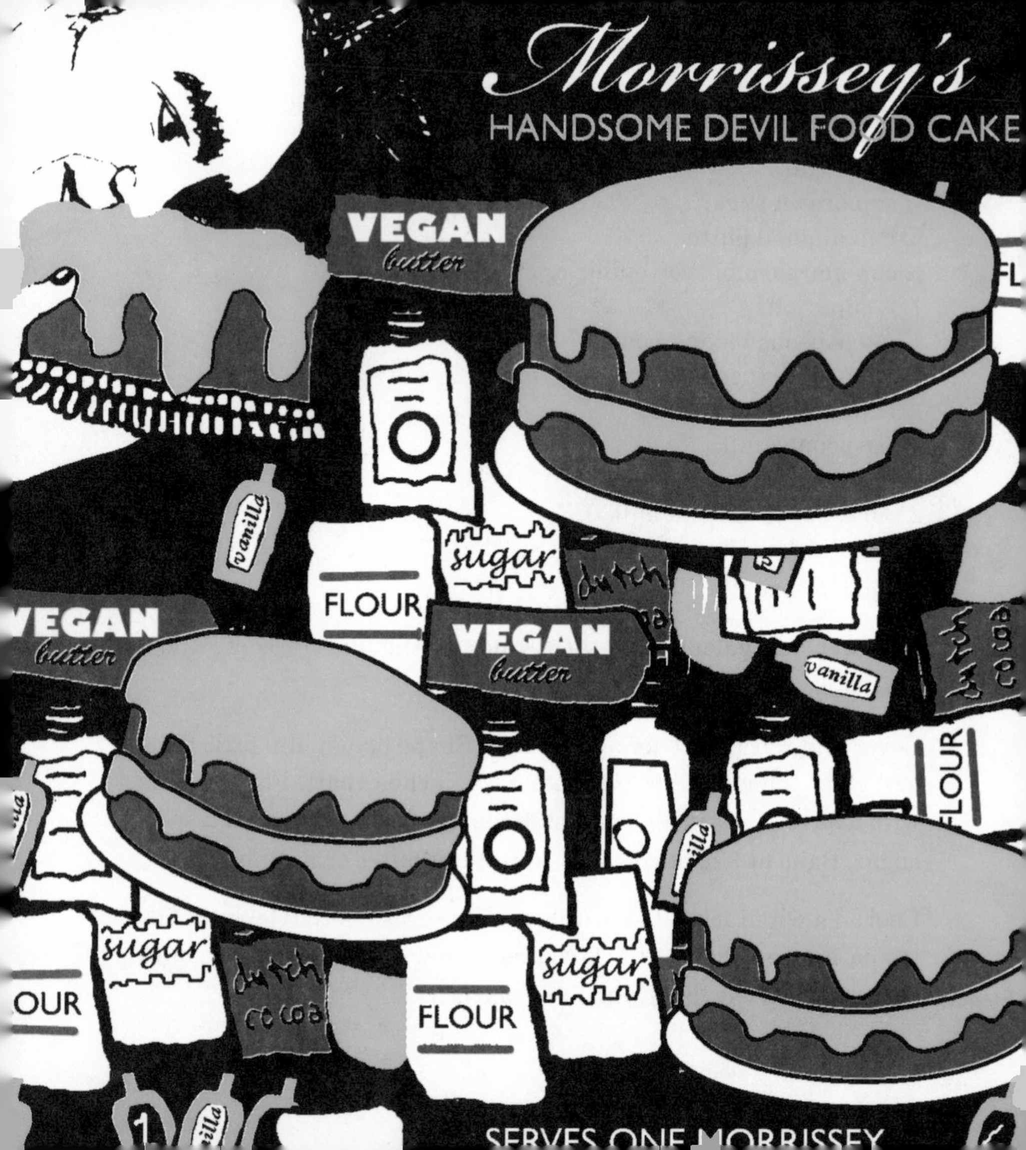
VEGAN
butter
vanilla
sugar
FLOUR
dutch cocoa
VEGAN
butter
VEGAN
butter
vanilla
FLOUR
sugar
dutch cocoa
sugar
FLOUR
OUR

SERVES ONE MORRISSEY

DEVIL FOOD CAKE

1 cup sugar

1 cup vegan sour cream

½ cup oil

¼ cup soy or other milk

1 teaspoon vanilla

1 ½ cups flour

½ cup cocoa powder

2 ½ teaspoons baking powder

A pinch of salt

Frosting:

½ cup margarine

2 ounces bittersweet chocolate, chopped

½ cup vegan cream cheese

¼ cup cocoa powder

1 teaspoon vanilla

2 cups powdered sugar, more or less

Mix together all of the dry ingredients for the cake, then stir in the wet. Add more liquid as needed for a nice cake batter consistency. Bake in two lightly greased or lined 8-inch cake pans at 350 degrees for 40 minutes, or until done. Don't jump around shouting, Come! Come! Come nuclear bomb!, or your cake may fall.

Melt chocolate and then combine it with the other frosting ingredients. Adjust by adding more powdered sugar or liquid as needed for the proper texture. Frost the two cakes and put them together, sealing the edges with more frosting, of course.

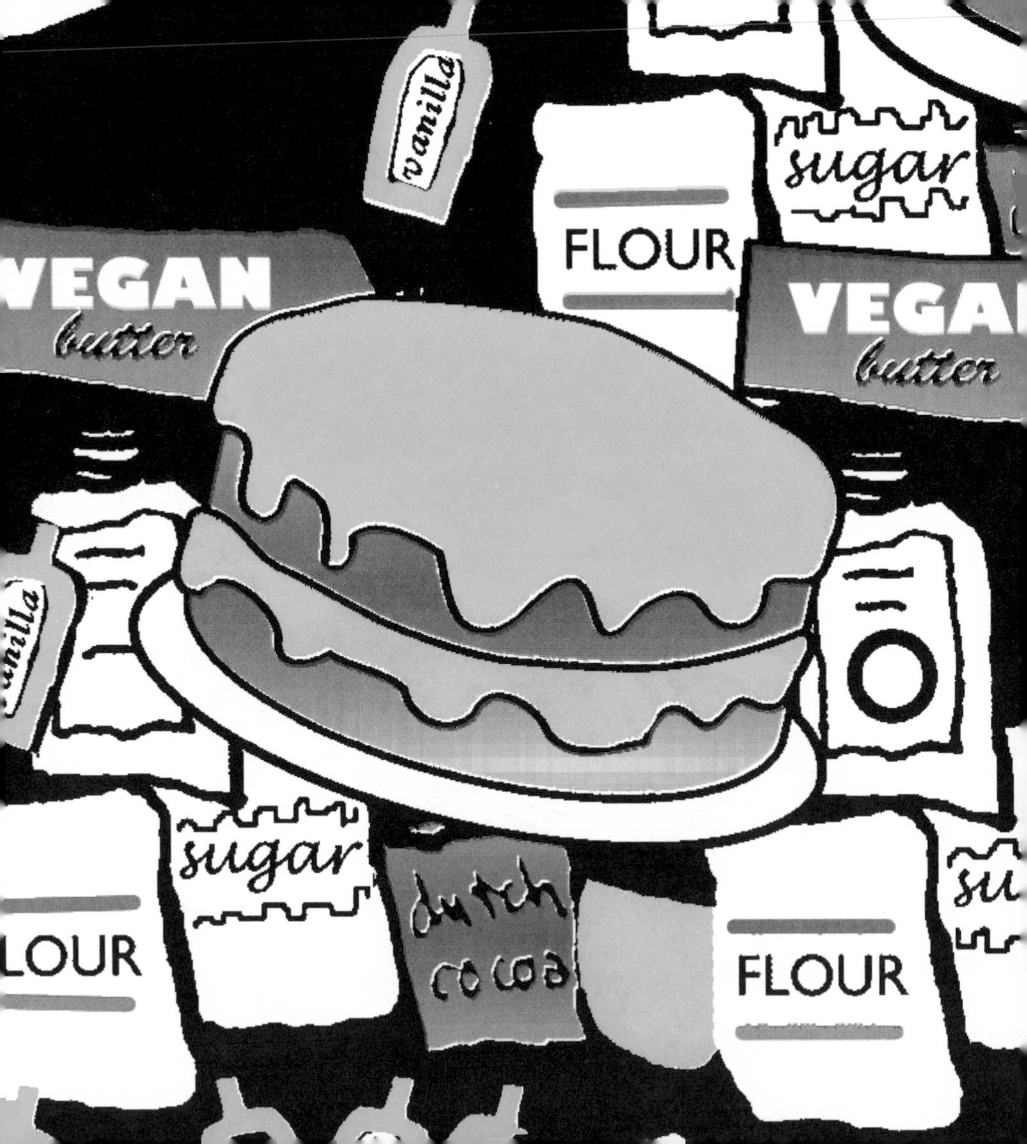
vanilla
sugar
FLOUR
VEGAN
butter
VEGAN
butter
vanilla
sugar
dutch
cocoa
LOUR
FLOUR

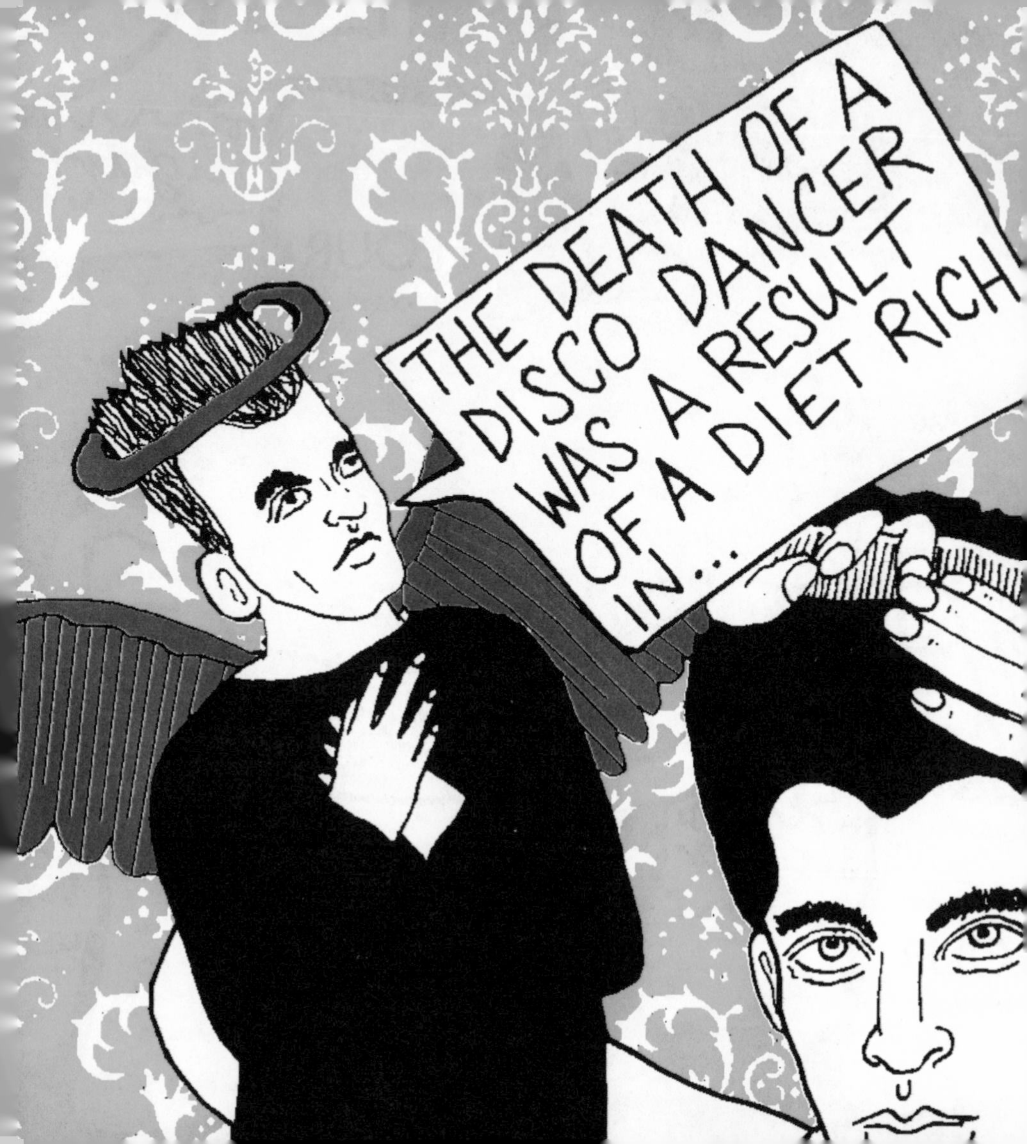
THE DEATH OF A DISCO DANCER WAS A RESULT OF A DIET RICH IN...

DISCO FRIES

2 or 3 cups french fries (cook them or go pick them up last)

1 cup cooked white beans (or tofu or potatoes)

2 tablespoons white miso

½ teaspoon cider vinegar

½ teaspoon agar flakes

3 to 4 garlic cloves, minced

1 teaspoon prepared mustard

Salt and white pepper, as desired

1 cup white onion, diced (it's getting pretty white around here!)

1 tablespoon tahini

½ cup soy or almond milk (more as needed)

2 cups mushroom broth

2 to 3 tablespoons flour

1 cup veggie chicken, chopped or shredded

Tamari or soy sauce, to taste

½ cup chopped mushrooms

¼ cup oil or margarine

Apparently, what makes this different from poutine is that instead of curds, it's melty cheese. And it's supposed to be chicken gravy. Poor twisted child: so ugly, so ugly. I'm not entirely a poutine fan myself, much preferring the ol' french-fry pie, where the fries and gravy are in a delicious pie crust with a buttload of caramelized onions on top.

Blend agar, white beans, soy milk, miso, mustard, vinegar, half of the onion, tahini, half the oil and half of the garlic. Heat until it bubbles, stirring. Remove from heat and whisk in vinegar. Set aside. If it gets too thick to glob or pour on, add more liquid.

Sauté the rest of the onion and garlic with vegan chicken and the rest of the oil. Add mushrooms and sprinkle with tamari.

Separately whisk flour into mushroom broth. Pour into pan with chiknun. Add salt and pepper to taste. Stir until it thickens a bit and seems tasty.

Pour mixture over french fries, and then smoother with cheeze sauce. If you like, you can do this in a pan and then broil the bastard for a few minutes.

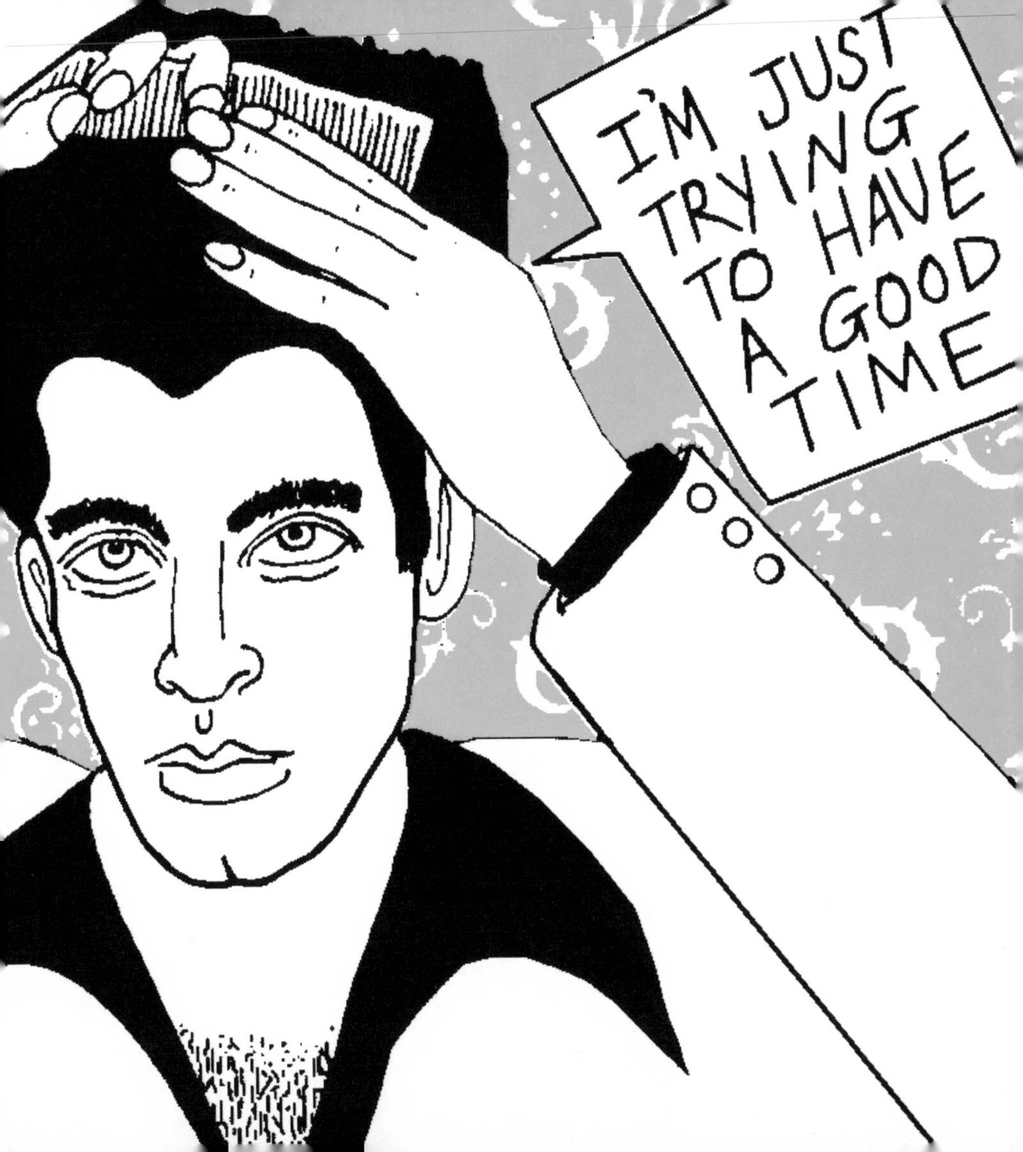
I'M JUST TRYING TO HAVE A GOOD TIME

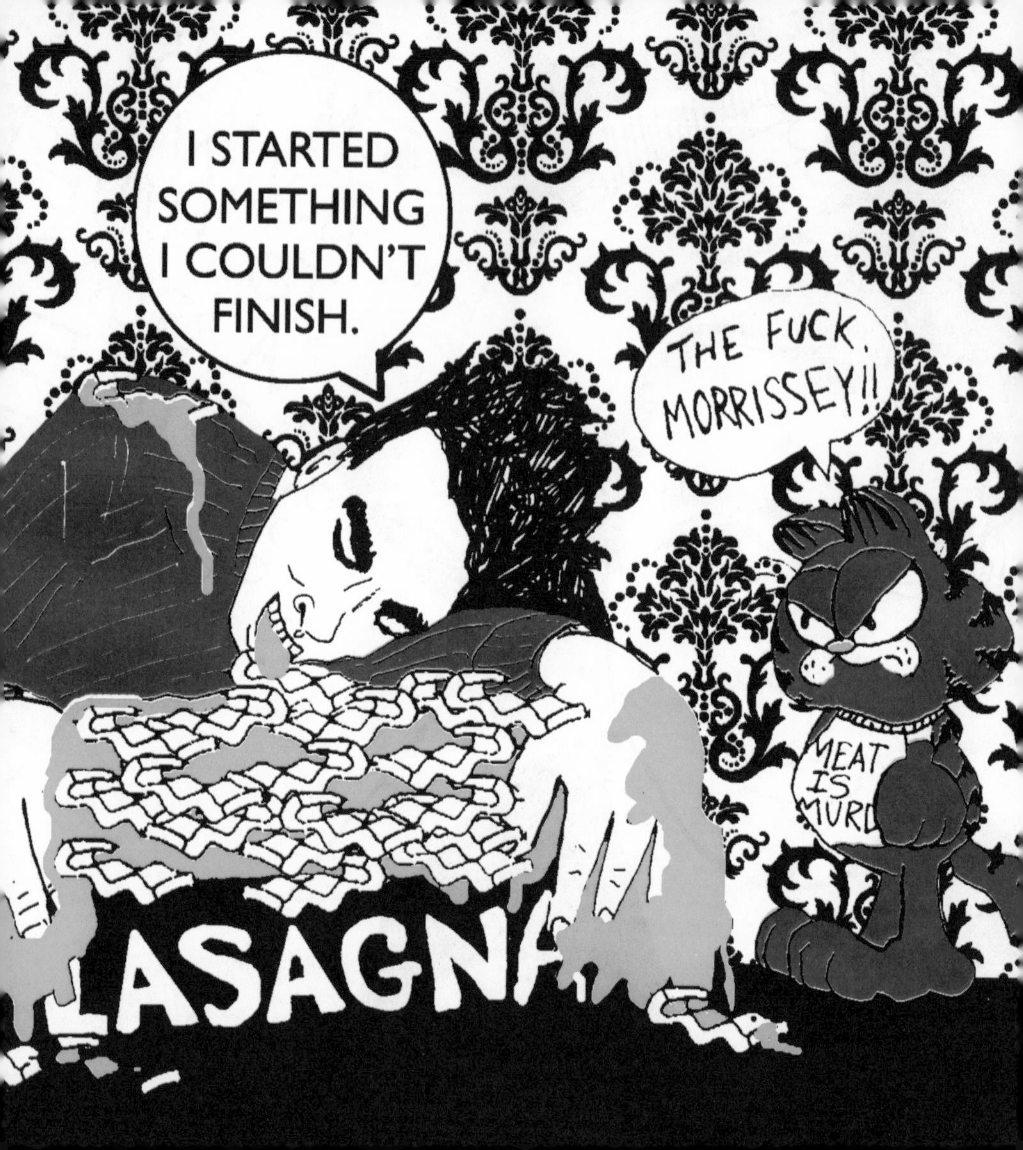
I STARTED SOMETHING I COULDN'T FINISH.
THE FUCK, MORRISSEY!!
MEAT IS MURD
LASAGNA

LASAGNA

3 cups roasted green tomatoes, chopped

½ cup basil leaves

A little broth

½ teaspoon ground coriander

Salt and black pepper, as needed or wanted (desired even)

Several upon several tablespoons olive oil

1 ½ cups shiitake mushrooms, sliced

1 ½ cups onions, diced

2 cups baby spinach

2 cups tofu, mashed potatoes, or cooked white beans

6 or 7 garlic cloves, minced

¼ cup nutritional yeast

1 cup favorite vegan cheeze (more if you like)

2 tablespoons tahini

A package or two lasagna noodles

1 tablespoon white balsamic vinegar

2 tablespoons lemon juice

1 or 2 tablespoons green curry paste

2 tablespoons white miso paste

White pepper, to taste

¼ cup Italian parsley, chopped

1 tablespoon brown mustard

Halve and roast tomatoes at 350 degrees with a little oil, salt, and black pepper for 45 minutes.

Boil the noodles until al dente, drain, and set aside. You can run cold water on them to stop continued cooking. I used to try to put them in uncooked, but I was young and foolish, and now am full of tears, for they were not "oven ready noodles." Do not be tempted to use those. Blech!

Puree green tomatoes with a little broth, 3 garlic cloves, salt and black pepper (to taste), basil, 2 tablespoons of olive oil, ¼ cup of the onion, white balsamic vinegar, coriander, and green curry paste. Should not be super runny.

Adjust seasonings to taste. Such a fun idea! (I'm sure I'm not the first to think of it.)

Mix together tofu (or potatoes or beans), lemon juice, nutritional yeast, salt and white pepper (to taste), 2 tablespoons olive oil, tahini, mustard, and miso. Add in parsley and set aside.

Sauté mushrooms, the rest of the onion, garlic, spinach, and whatever else you want with salt, pepper, and Italian herbs to taste. Set aside. I know this seems a little complicated. Have confidence and you can get it all done. Keats and Yeats are on your side.

It's time to put it all together now! In a greased lasagna pan (a.k.a. a baking or casserole dish, you silly billy!), place down a little of the sauce (only a few tablespoons), then lay down a layer of noodles. Follow this with the tofu concoction, and then a little sauce. Add another layer of noodles, drizzle these with a bit of oil, then add the sauteed veggies and a bit of sauce. And then another layer of noodles. Pour the rest of the sauce over this and sprinkle with vegan cheese.

Bake at 375 degrees for 45 minutes or until done to your liking.

Could be a favorite dish, of deities or mortals, or of both!

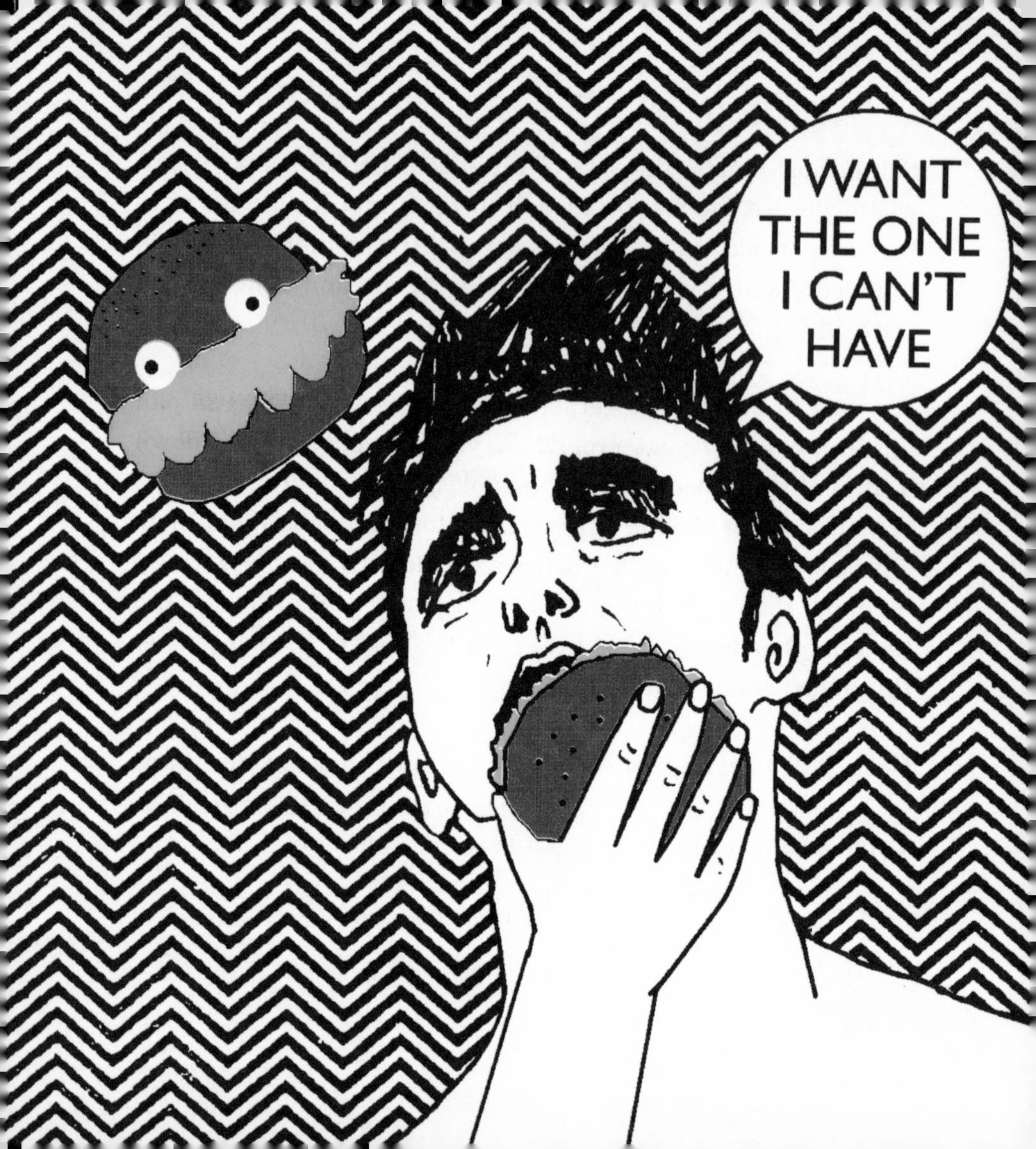
I WANT THE ONE I CAN'T HAVE

MUSHROOM BURGER

1 ½ cups dried mushrooms, in pieces (can mix any you like)

½ cup chopped fresh mushrooms

¼ cup mushroom broth (more as needed)

A little cornstarch or potato starch

3 or 4 tablespoons tapioca flour

2 tablespoon tamari (more as needed)

Salt and black pepper

2 or 3 tablespoons oil plus some for sauté

¼ cup chopped onion

2 or 3 garlic cloves, minced

A little minced rosemary

In a food processor, grind down those dried mushrooms further—to a coarse powder, if possible. (Mushroom flour is something that ought to be used more.)

Combine with the other ingredients, adding a little more liquid or starch as needed to make a modestly sticky dough. Form patties with your hands and cook them in a griddle or other suitable pan with light oil, turning once until browned on both sides.

Cover with an assortment of fixings, scavenging through life's very constant lulls. Recommended: pickled or caramelized red onion, fried pickles, crispy garlic, arugula, green tomatoes, tater tots, mango chutney, HP sauce, pesto mayo...

Don't forget to toast those buns!!

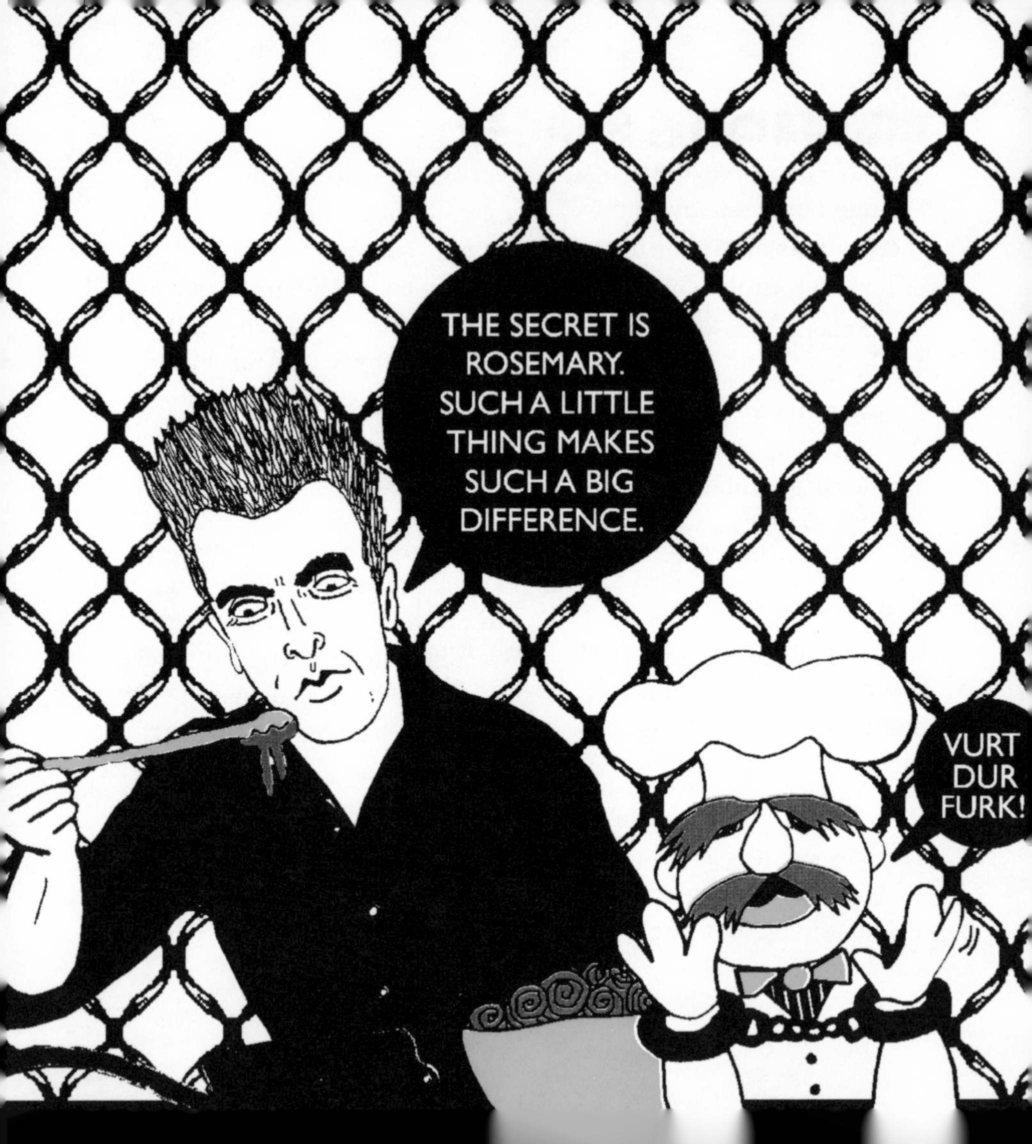
THE SECRET IS ROSEMARY. SUCH A LITTLE THING MAKES SUCH A BIG DIFFERENCE.
VURT DUR FURK!

ROSEMARY

Several sprigs rosemary

1 cup lemon juice

½ cup sugar syrup (or to taste)

Several handfuls borage flowers

2 teaspoons rosewater

4 cups water

(Double this all for a more substantial amount)

Mix water, sugar syrup, rosewater, and lemon juice together. Crush a couple sprigs of rosemary and stir them in.

Add some borage flowers. Allow everything to chill for a few hours. Stir again and serve with ice, garnishing with more rosemary and borage. It's so simple, you'll kick yourself for never having thought of it before—you may well, it's really laughable!

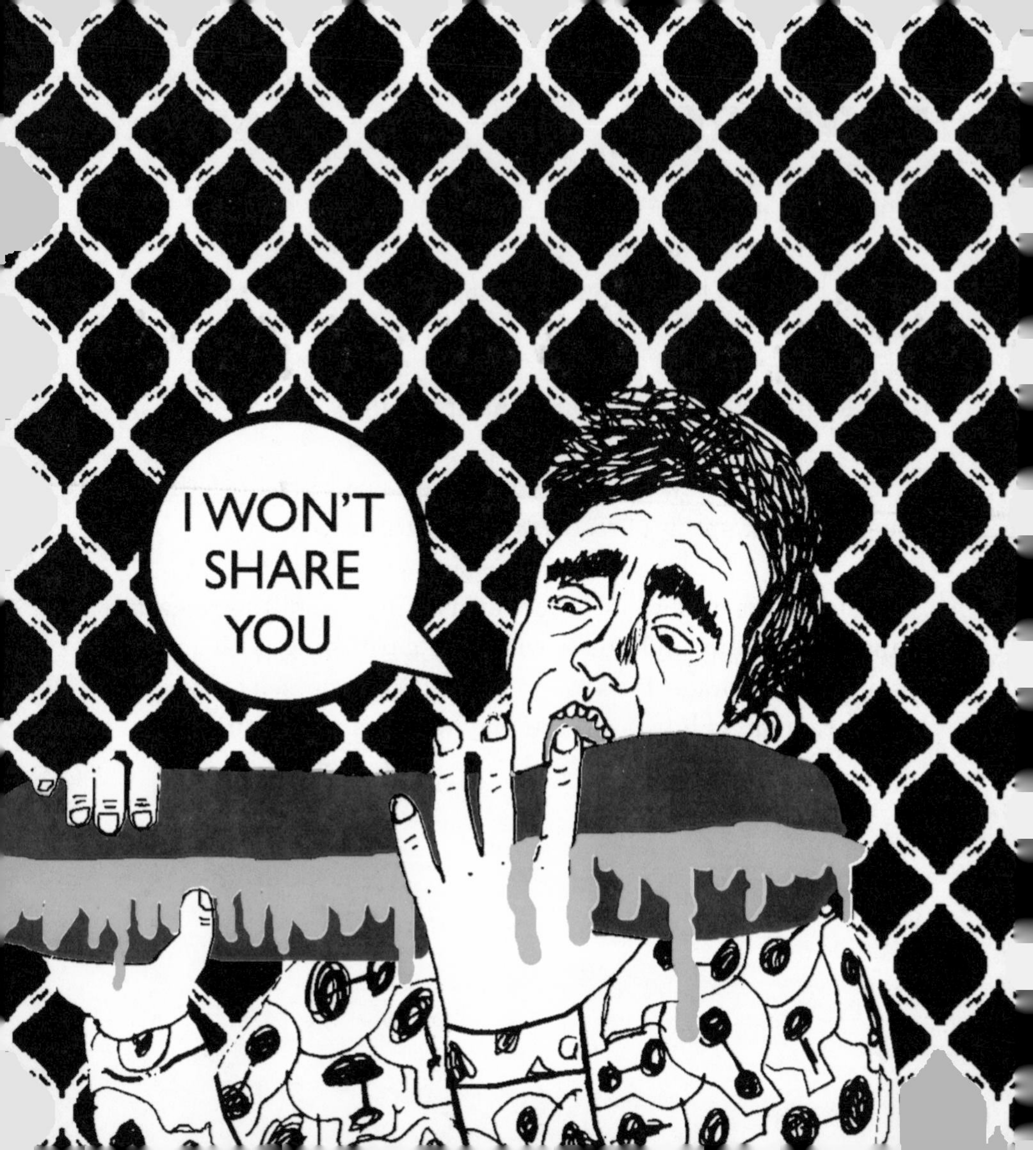
I WON'T SHARE YOU

SANDWICH

12 half moon slices of eggplant about ¼ inches thick
2 teaspoons curry powder
Salt to taste
½ cup flour or rice flour
1 cup onions, sliced
½ cup red bell peppers, sliced
2 garlic cloves
½ cup artichoke hearts
1 or 2 tablespoons sriracha or favorite chili sauce
2 tablespoons lemon juice
¼ cup olive oil
¼ cup herbs (I'd go basil, oregano, and dill)
Several slices tomatoes
Arugula to garnish

Blend artichoke hearts, olive oil, lemon juice, sriracha, garlic, herbs, and a little salt to taste. Set aside.

Saute onion in a little oil with salt to taste until browned. Set aside.

Salt the eggplant lightly and drizzle with oil. Mix flour, salt, and curry powder together. Add water or soda water to make a pancake batter-ish consistency, and dredge the eggplant pieces in this. Then fry them in light oil, turning once, until browned. Put together with tomatoes, arugula, sauteed onions, and artichoke spread to make the delicious sandwich.

You're probably wondering what sort of bread to use. I would recommend baguette or other grinder-style bread for this. A crack on the head is what you get for not asking.

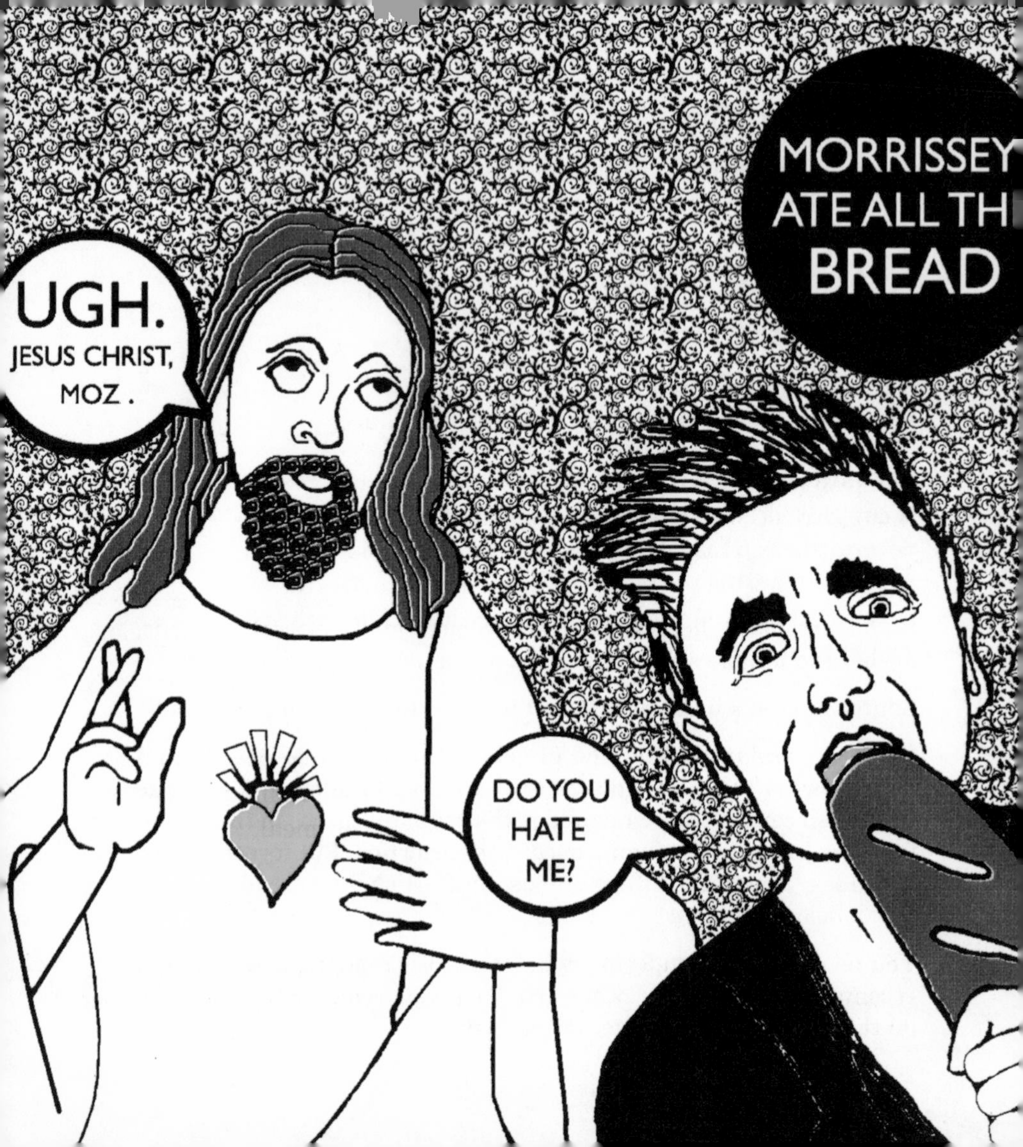
MORRISSEY ATE ALL TH BREAD
UGH. JESUS CHRIST, MOZ.
DO YOU HATE ME?

BREAD

4 or 4 ½ cups flour
1 envelope dry active yeast
1 teaspoon baking powder
1 ½ teaspoons salt
2 tablespoons olive oil
1 ½ cups warm water
1 tablespoon sugar
A few tablespoons cornmeal

Activate yeast in warm water with sugar (about 10 minutes), and stir. Add oil, salt, and baking powder, and then slowly work in flour to make a kneadable dough. Use more or less flour as needed. Work on a floured board for several minutes to make a smooth ball. Grease the ball lightly, place in a large bowl, and cover loosely with a light towel.

Allow dough to rise until it has doubled and the air hangs heavy like a dulling wine (about an hour and a half: maybe less, maybe more). Punch down and divide in two. Knead each half on floured board, make into oblong shape, and dust with cornmeal.

Place in two lightly oiled, large loaf pans, or baguette or other form pans, and allow to rise for an hour or so yet again. Bake at 375 degrees for about 35 to 40 minutes, or until crusty and you can thump it a good one. A sort of bouncy, hollow thump should answer.

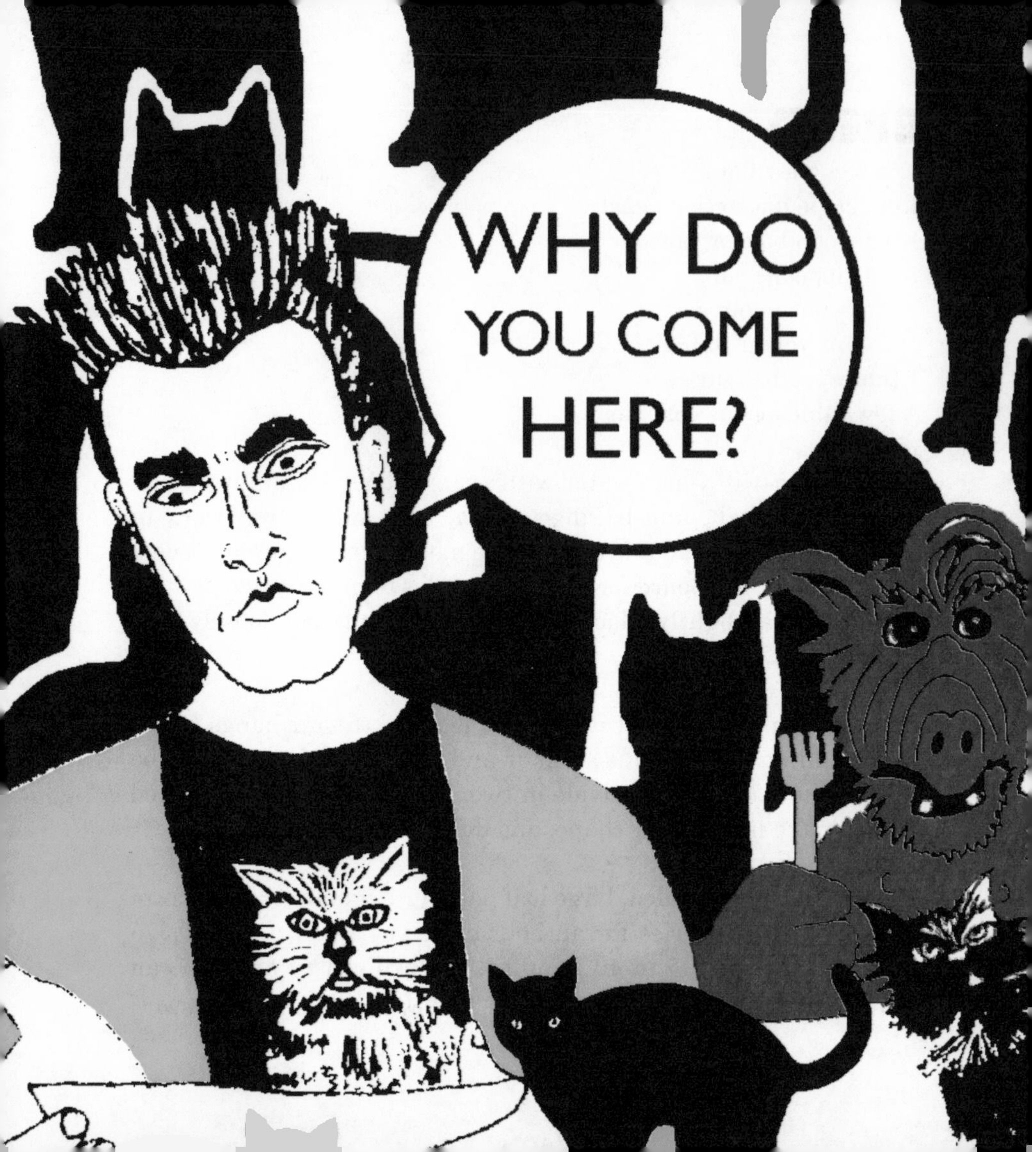
WHY DO YOU COME HERE?

ALFCATS

½ cup brown sugar

⅓ cup margarine or coconut oil

½ cup dark molasses for dark cats or corn syrup for light cats

½ cup water or vegan milk

3 or 3 ½ cups flour (more as needed)

1 teaspoon baking soda

1 ½ teaspoons ground ginger

½ teaspoon ground allspice

½ teaspoon ground cloves

1 teaspoon ground cinnamon

¼ teaspoon salt

Cat-shaped cookie cutter

Also helpful:

A batch of icing, your favorite type (maybe some chocolate and some plain)

Flaked coconut

Cinnamon or shaved chocolate

Other colorful additions

You may have loved ALF, hated ALF, or never heard of ALF. He ate a steady diet of cats and this truth is a central part of your mind's landscape whether you care or do not.

Mix brown sugar, shortening, molasses, and water in a bowl. Mix in flour, baking soda, ginger, allspice, cloves, cinnamon, and salt to form nice cookie dough, adding more flour or liquid if needed. Cover and refrigerate for 2 to 3 hours or until firm. Roll out dough in batches ¼ inches thick on a floured surface. Cut with a floured, cat cookie cutter. Place about 2 inches apart on lightly greased or parchment-lined cookie sheets.

Bake 10 to 12 minutes at 350 degrees or until done. Cool on wire rack.

Frost if you like, adding coconut, cinnamon, or chocolate to the top to make a variety of different, tasty looking cats that ALF would approve of.

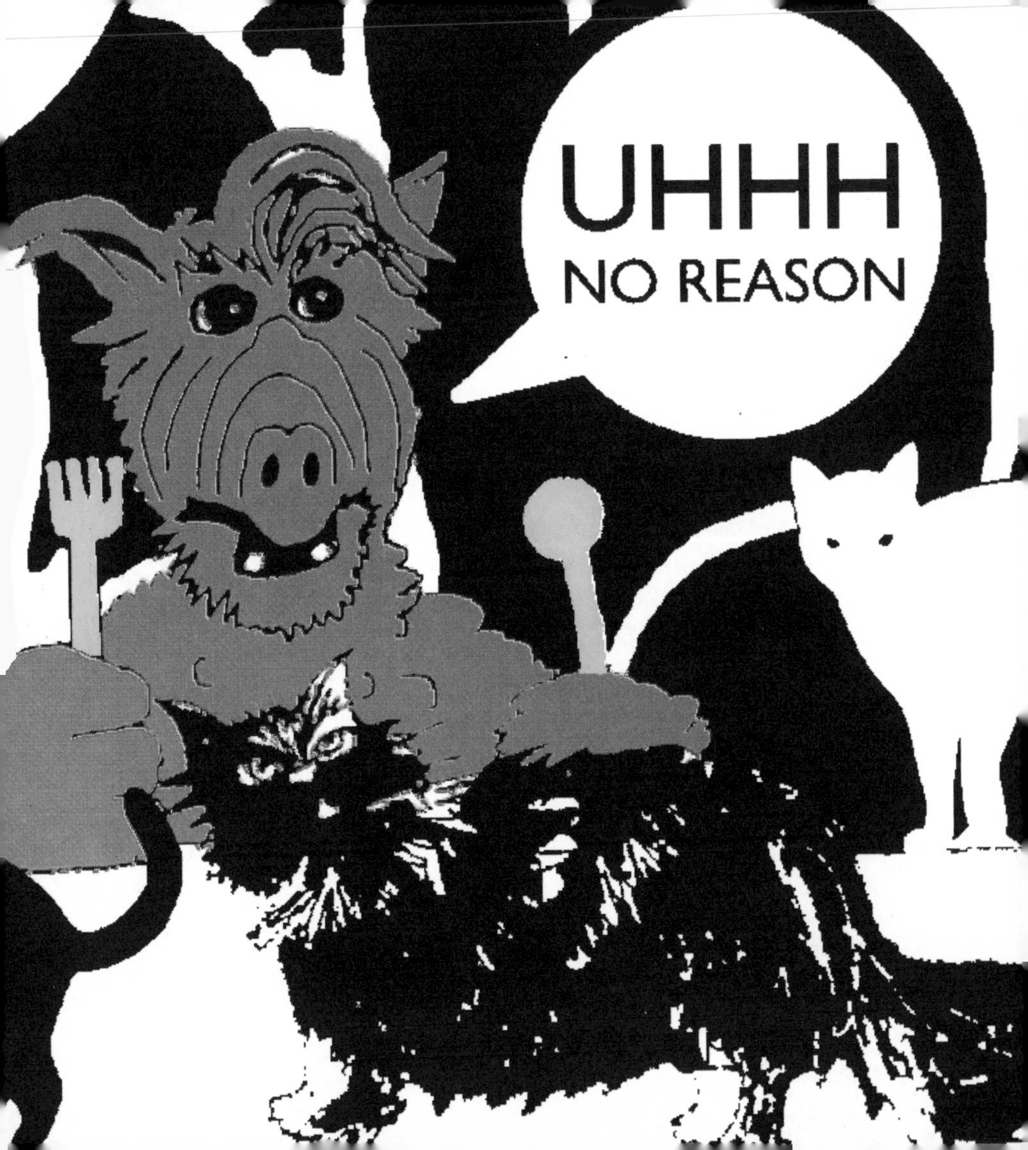
UHHH
NO REASON

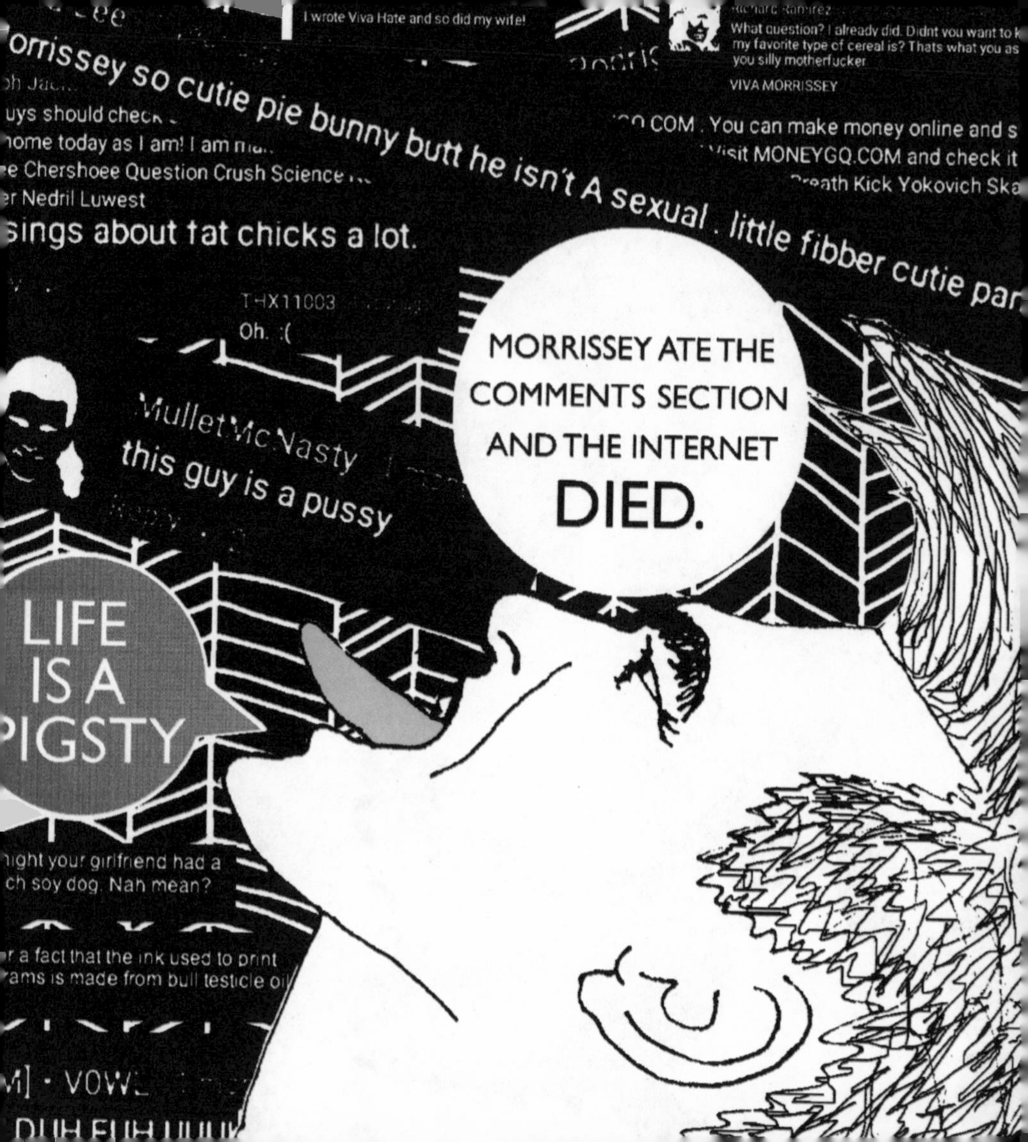
I wrote Viva Hate and so did my wife!
What question? I already did. Didnt you want to k
my favorite type of cereal is? Thats what you as
you silly motherfucker
VIVA MORRISSEY
orrissey so cutie pie bunny butt he isn't A sexual . little fibber cutie par
uys should check
home today as I am! I am
e Chershoee Question Crush Science
r Nedril Luwest
COM . You can make money online and s
isit MONEYGQ.COM and check it
reath Kick Yokovich Ska
sings about fat chicks a lot.
THX11003
Oh. :(
MulletMcNasty
this guy is a pussy
MORRISSEY ATE THE COMMENTS SECTION AND THE INTERNET DIED.
LIFE IS A PIGSTY
ight your girlfriend had a
ch soy dog. Nah mean?
r a fact that the ink used to print
ams is made from bull testicle oi
M] · VOW

INTERNET

Spaghetti for two

Favorite beans of choice (like a cup or so, cooked, mixed with salt and pepper and a nice spice or herb blend)

½ pound okra

A couple teaspoons chili powder

2 onions, diced

4 to 5 garlic cloves, minced

Margarine or coconut oil, to taste

2 tablespoons tomato paste

¼ cup chili sauce

½ cup barbecue sauce

1 pound ground tempeh

1 teaspoon chili powder

½ teaspoon cumin

½ teaspoon ground coriander

1 teaspoon smoked paprika

½ cup white beans

2 to 3 tablespoons miso

¼ cup nutritional yeast

$1/_3$ cup cashew or other milk

Salt and pepper

Oil to fry okra, plus several tablespoons for everything else... Oil! Oil! Oil!

A little flour or cornmeal

½ cup green bell pepper, chopped

1 cup olives, chopped

¼ cup red bell pepper, minced

½ teaspoon thyme, minced
1 to 2 tablespoons balsamic vinegar
2 roma tomatoes, seeded and minced (or chopped very small)
Arugula for topping

Five-Way Chili is a Cincinnati concoction of beans, chili, cheese, spaghetti, and onions. The Internet is more like an Eight-Way Chili, and Morrissey has little or nothing to do with Cincinnati, much like the Internet has usually little to do with whatever you actually want it to be doing.

So here we go with spaghetti, beans, uncheez, onions, fried okra, chili, tapenade, and, um, arugula. This is a surprising combination! And, of course, you remember the last time I tried to surprise you: I crept up behind you with a homeless chihuahua. This is a lot like that.

Mix olives with a little onion, some garlic, thyme, salt and pepper, red bell pepper, tomatoes, and a little olive oil. Set aside or put in fridge. Truffle oil is also good in this stuff.

Sauté tempeh with salt and pepper in a little oil. Add one of the onions and a little garlic, and cook until tempeh is browned. Add smoked paprika, chili powder, tomato paste, coriander, cumin, and green bell pepper, and stir.

Cook 2 to 3 minutes, then add chili sauce, a little broth or water, and barbecue sauce. Cook for 5 to 10 minutes, adjusting seasonings to taste.

Blend nutritional yeast, white beans, miso, and "milk." Season to taste. Cook over low heat until slightly thickened, stirring. Set aside.

Slice okra and coat with flour or cornmeal with some salt and chili powder mixed in. Fry in hot oil until browned, and drain on absorbent paper.

Make sure your spaghetti and beans are also ready.

Fry the other chopped onion in some oil with a splash of balsamic. Add a little salt and pepper and cook until they start to brown or caramelize. Add any remaining garlic and cook for a couple minutes. Add spaghetti and toss with margarine. Add the beans.

Remove from heat. Plate some of this spaghetti/onions/beans concoction, pile on some chili, add okra, and uncheezy sauce, followed by a dollop of tapenade and a scatter of arugula. Or do it in whatever order you like.

Drizzle with a tahini balsamic and truffle oil.

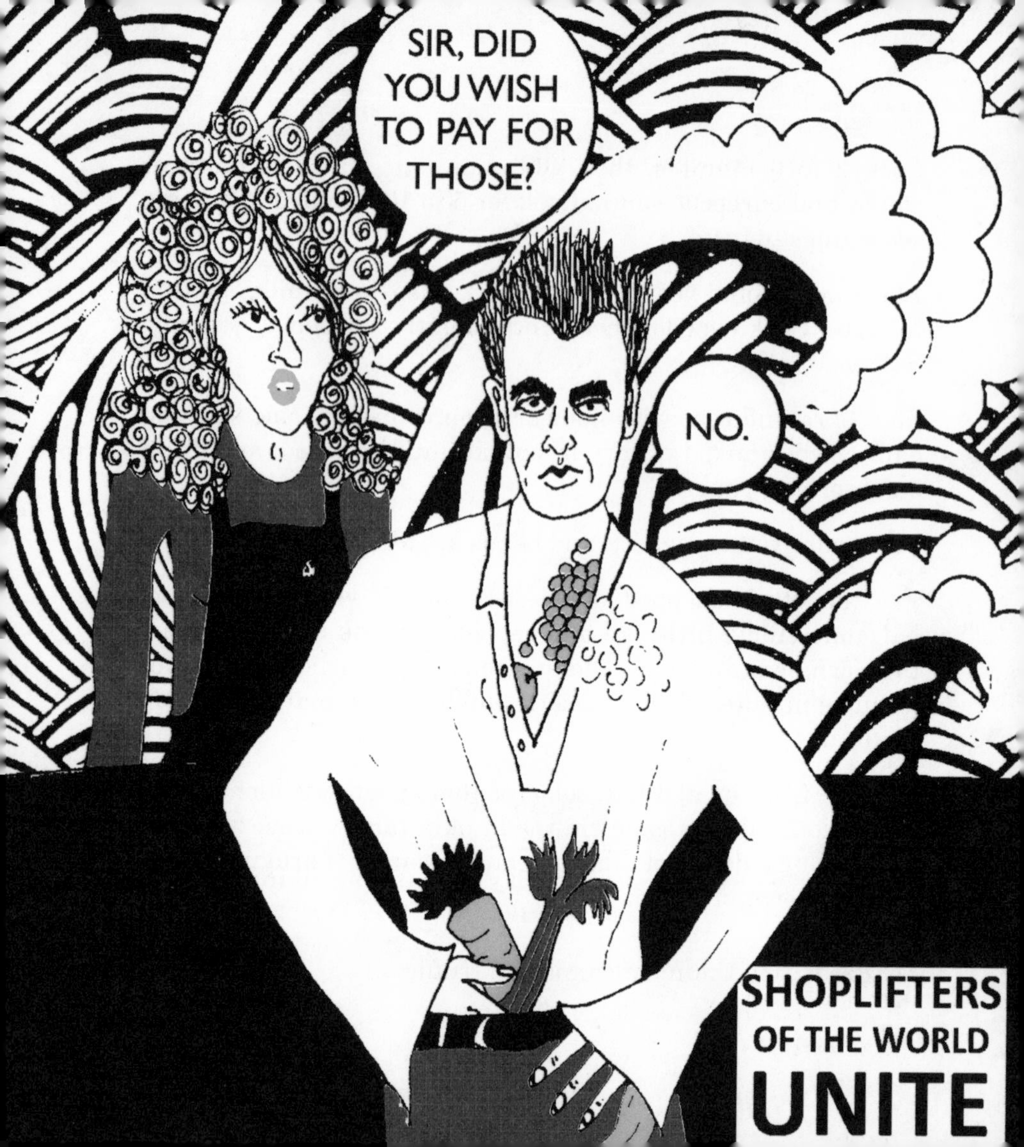
SIR, DID YOU WISH TO PAY FOR THOSE?
NO.
SHOPLIFTERS OF THE WORLD UNITE

VEGGIES

1 pound Brussels sprouts, split

2 carrots, cut into 1-inch rounds

1 red bell pepper, cut into strips

1 pound sweet potatoes, cut into 1-inch cubes

1 red onion, cut into large chunks

Salt and pepper to taste

8 garlic cloves

2 or 3 tablespoons olive oil

Smoked paprika

A few bits of fresh rosemary

2 tablespoons balsamic reduction

You probably thought I would have you make something overly complicated, but oh, I'm not the man you think I am.

Toss veggies with garlic, oil, paprika, and rosemary. Place in a baking dish. Begin baking at 375 degrees for 25 minutes, then toss, season again, drizzle with balsamic reduction, and bake for another 15 minutes or until it's done to your liking.

Makes a modest side dish.

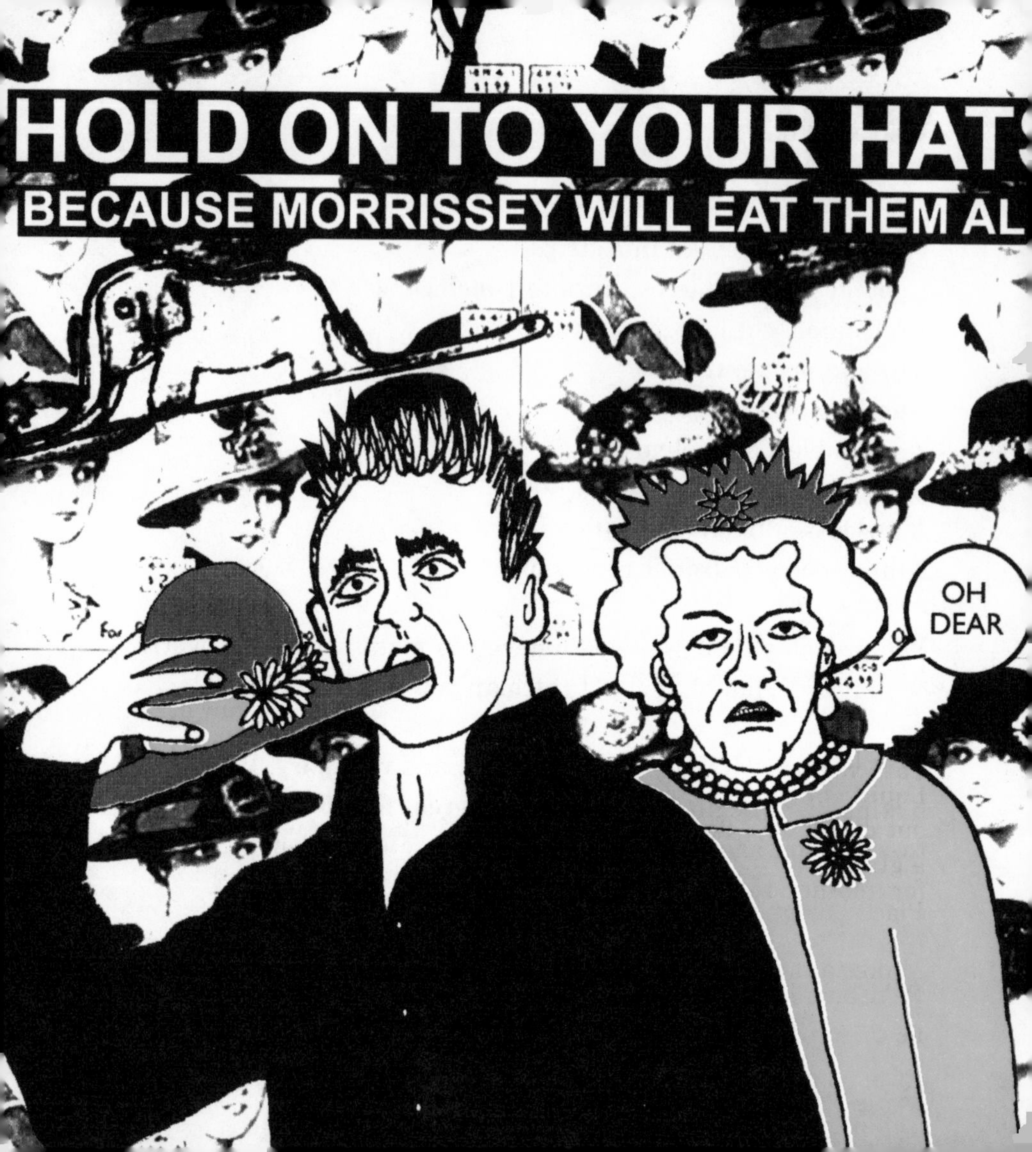
HOLD ON TO YOUR HAT
BECAUSE MORRISSEY WILL EAT THEM AL
OH DEAR

HATS

2 cups flour
2 ¼ teaspoons baking powder
½ cup sugar
½ cup margarine or coconut oil
¼ teaspoon salt
¼ cup coconut cream, or silken tofu blended with ¼ cup vegan milk
½ teaspoon vanilla
½ teaspoon almond extract

Filling:

1 cup apricot jam
½ cup prunes or golden raisins, chopped
½ teaspoon lemon juice
2 tablespoons sugar

I've gone with Hamantaschen for this challenge—it is someone's hat, after all. You may have expected a brimmed hat, but no. So don't be too jaded to question stagnation. The world has many hats.

In a large bowl, mix dry ingredients. Cut in margarine/oil. Add liquid and extracts, and mix well to form dough into a ball. Roll out dough on a floured surface and cut into circles using a can or a glass.

Place dollop of filling in center of each circle and pull up three edges to form a triangle. Pinch the edges together up top to seal.

Bake on a lightly greased or parchment-lined sheet at 350 degrees for 25 minutes or until lightly browned.

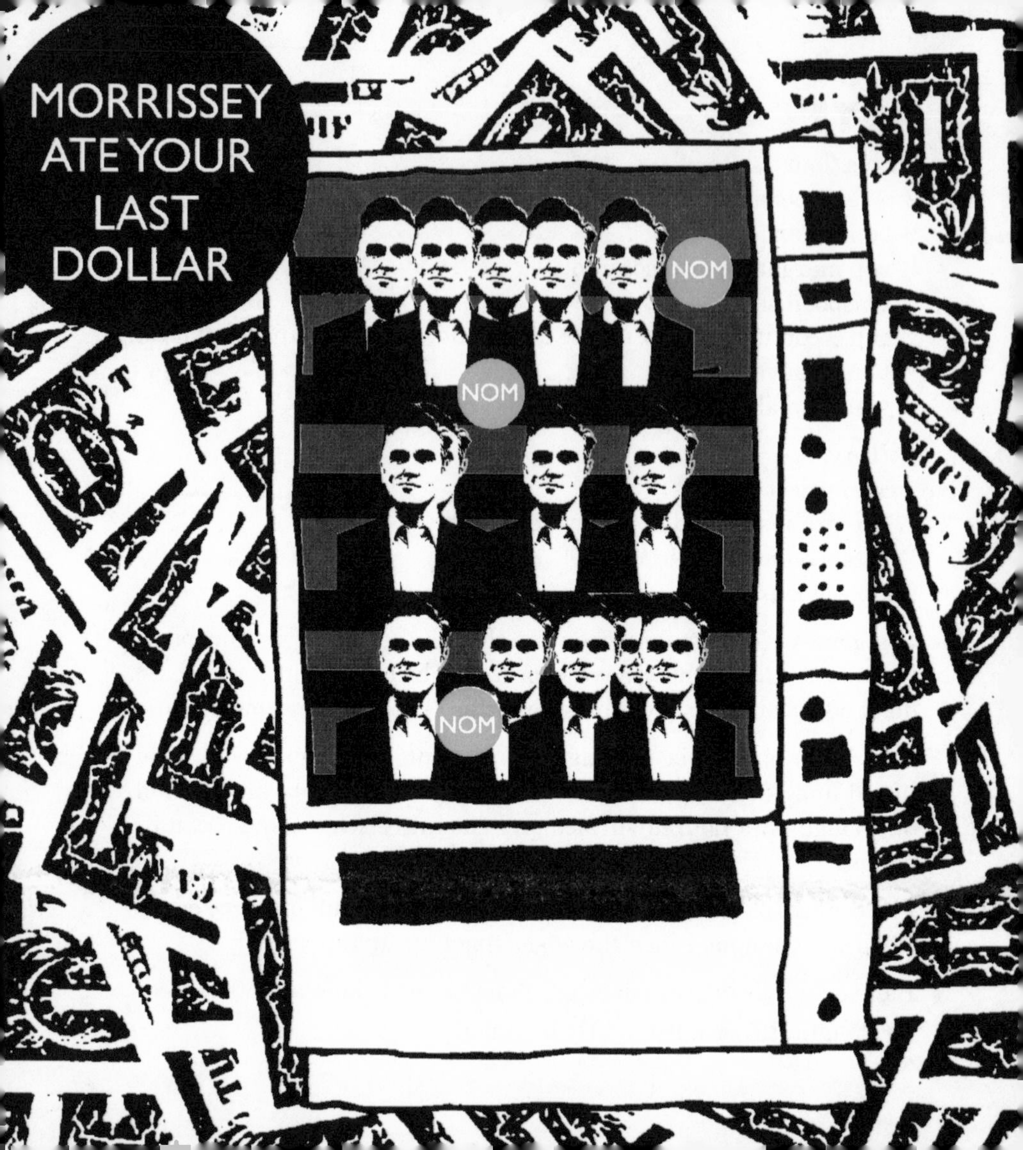
MORRISSEY
ATE YOUR
LAST
DOLLAR
NOM
NOM
NOM

LAST DOLLAR

2 cups sifted flour
2 ½ teaspoon baking powder
2 or 3 tablespoons sugar
½ teaspoon salt
2 teaspoons cornstarch or tapioca flour
1 ½ cup favorite vegan milk (personally, I would go cashew on this one)
$^1/_3$ cup silken tofu or coconut cream (or apple sauce)
3 tablespoons margarine or coconut oil, melted

Everyone loves pancakes. Isn't it a bummer when you make pancakes for your friends in the morning and "someone" doesn't want any?! Rejection is one thing but rejection from a fool is cruel.

If you make these with water instead of milk, it may really only cost your last dollar. Mix dry ingredients together, and then mix in the wet. Cook in a skillet in small dollops, allowing batter to spread a little to form...dun dunh dunh...dollar cakes of course. Cook until lightly browned on both sides. Just lightly oil the pan unless you want crispy fried ones.

Ways to jazz these up: add curry powder, garlic, onions/scallions, maybe some shredded sweet potato to the batter, and serve with gravy, sour kreem, salsa, or something else appropriate for delicious, savory, baby pancakes. In this case, definitely fry the little suckers up.

Or add vanilla, maple sugar, blueberries, bananas, pecans, or other fun nuts or fruit, and serve with coconut cream, jam, molasses, and all sorts of things!

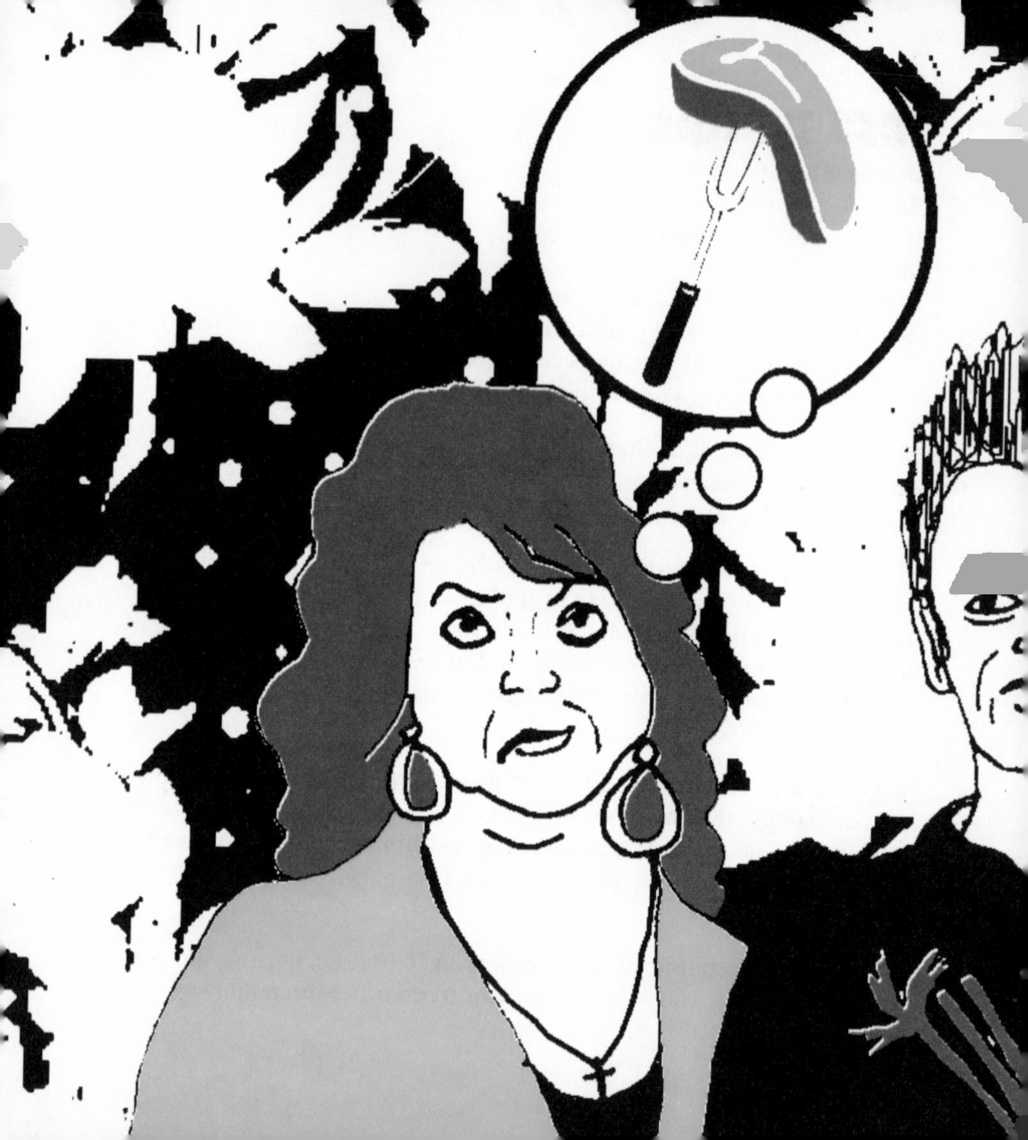

PAULA DEEN

2 ¼ cups flour, sifted

½ cup margarine, shortening or coconut oil

More margarine, mixed with 1 tablespoon minced chives and
formed into 12 little balls and frozen

1 ¼ cup vegan creamer or coconut milk (with cream)

1 tablespoon sugar

2 teaspoons cider vinegar

1 teaspoon onion powder

2 teaspoons baking powder

Many strips (12) veggie bacon, fried up

1 cup (or more) vegan cream cheez, seasoned to be more decadent

Salt and pepper, to taste

Here's a sweet biscuit stuffed with a veggie bacon and cream cheez, and a wrapped butter ball. Pretty much epitomizes her whole oeuvre to me.

Mix together flour, salt, sugar, baking powder, and onion powder. Add in margarine to make crumbs. Slowly add in creamer and make into a dough, adjust seasonings to taste. Add black pepper if you like. Roll into 12 balls and freeze.

Wrap each frozen margarine-chive ball in a strip of veggie bacon. Coat these with some of that vegan cream cheez. This may be sounding a bit decadent, but hey, life is a pigsty and we're wallowing in it with your good friend here.

Now take these and place in the center of each ball of dough. Flatten them a bit with your hand, making certain that they are sealed. Place on greased baking sheet and baste lightly with a mix of melted margarine and vegan creamer: once at the beginning, and once a few minutes before the end of baking.

Bake at 450 degrees for 15 to 20 minutes or so, keeping an eye on them so they don't burn.

Baste again when they come out of the oven.

Cover in gravy.

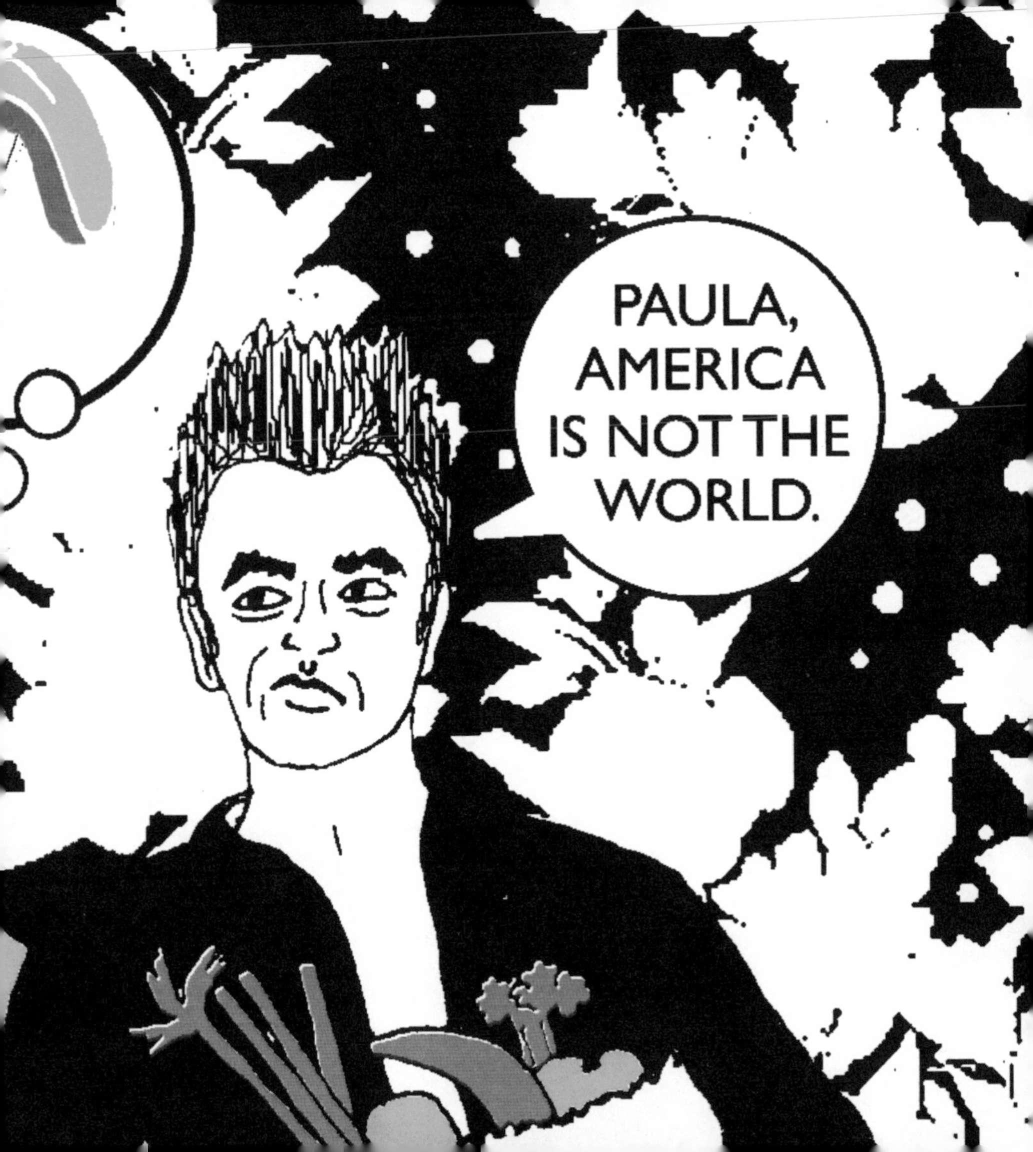
PAULA, AMERICA IS NOT THE WORLD.

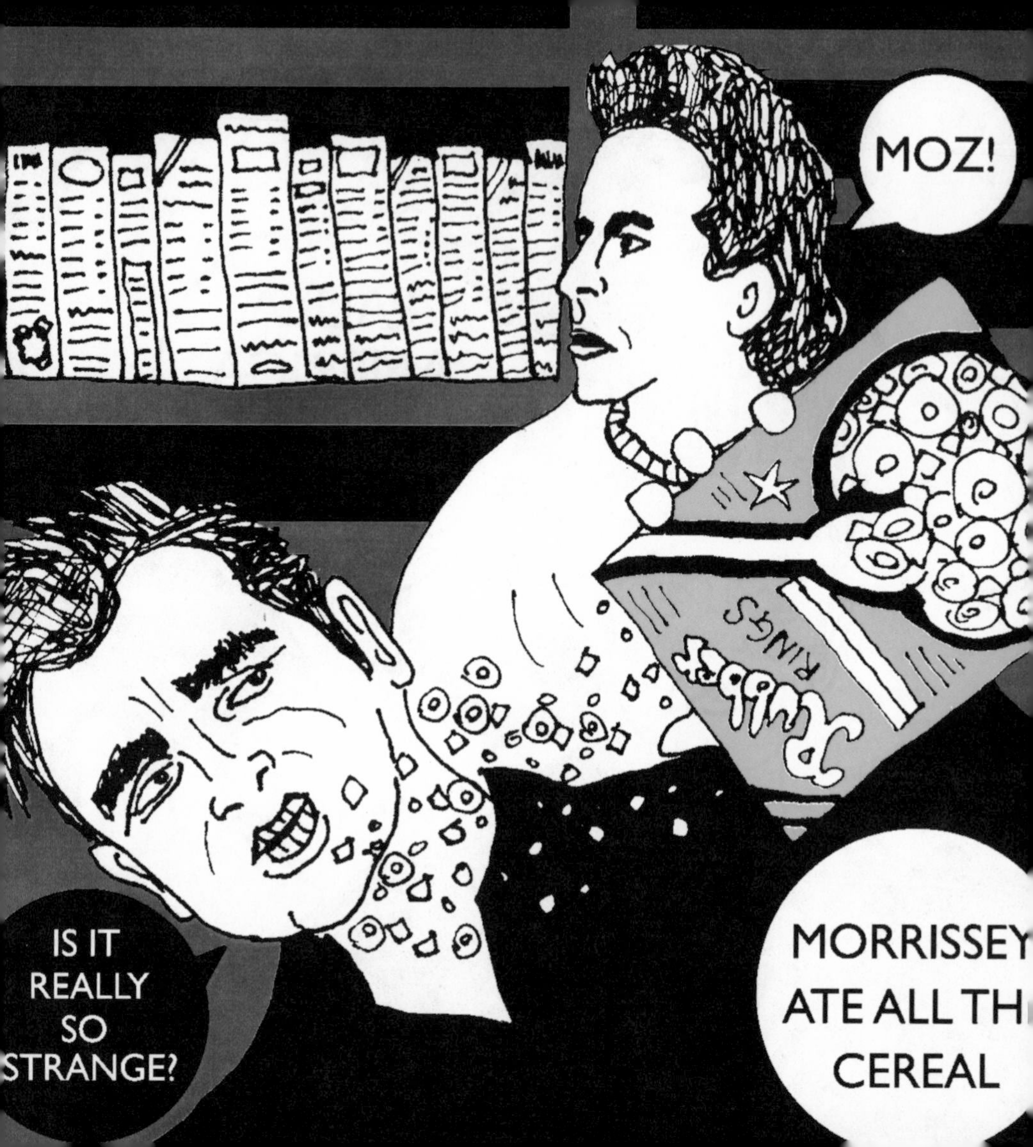
MOZ!
RINGS
IS IT REALLY SO STRANGE?
MORRISSEY ATE ALL TH CEREAL

CEREAL

1 cup oats
½ cup quinoa
½ cup walnuts
½ cup pecans
Salt and sugar, to taste
A few teaspoons oil
½ cup dried cranberries
½ cup golden raisins
¼ cup flax seeds

Cook quinoa til barely done, then drain and cool. Lay out flat on a baking sheet. Lay oats mixed with some salt, sugar, and oil on another baking sheet. Bake at 350 degrees, turning occasionally, for 15 minutes.

Add nuts and flax seeds, and then toast, turning occasionally, for another 10 minutes or so, being careful not to burn any of it. You can add whatever else you like: money, jewelry, or flesh.

Add dried cranberries and raisins, and enjoy with favorite milks.

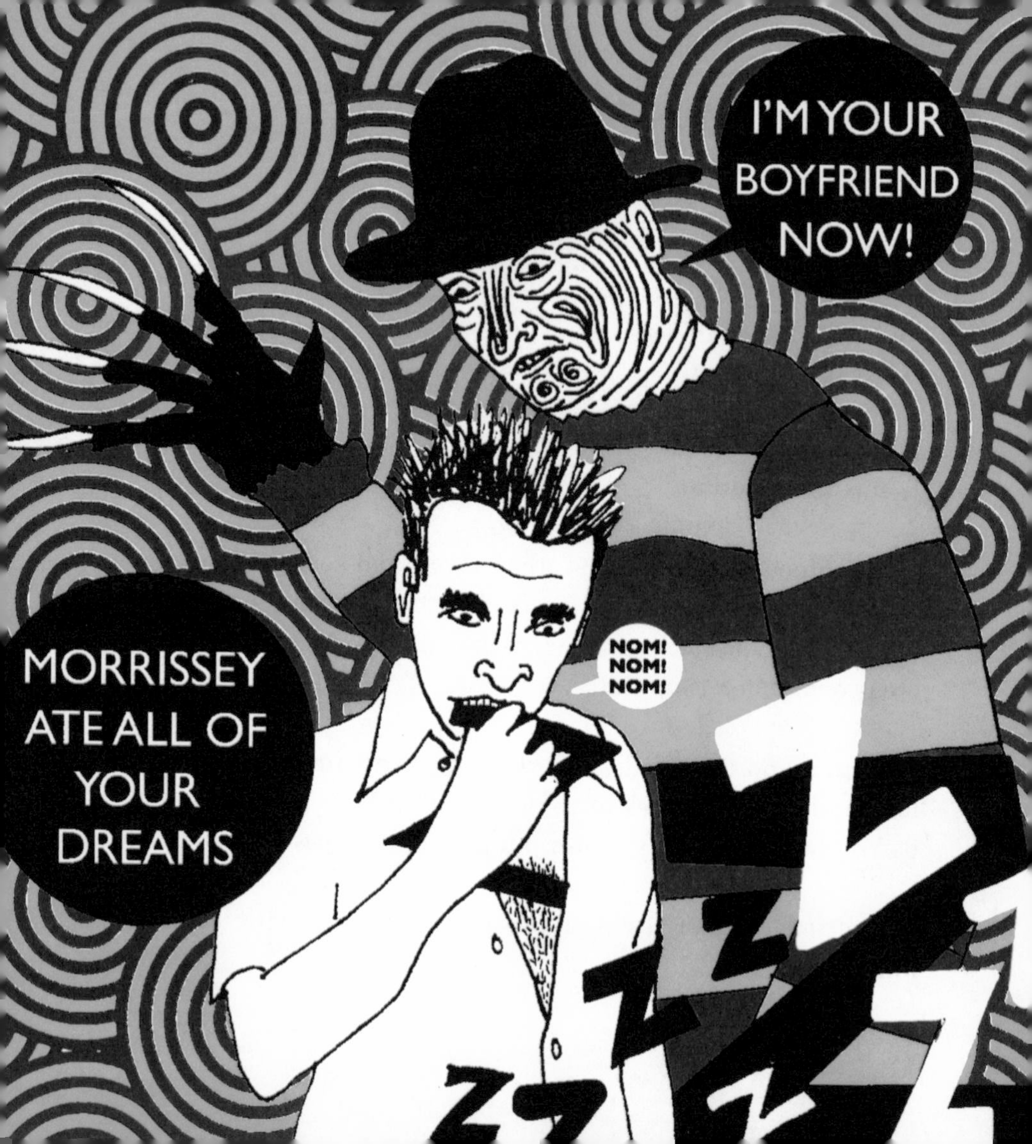
I'M YOUR BOYFRIEND NOW!
MORRISSEY ATE ALL OF YOUR DREAMS
NOM! NOM! NOM!

DREAMSICLE

1 cup coconut milk

2 or 3 tablespoons powdered sugar

1 teaspoon tapioca starch

(Blend it all up!)

Mix Separately

1 cup orange juice

1 cup coconut cream or milk

½ teaspoon vanilla

¼ cup powdered sugar (more to taste)

You need popsicle sticks and molds

Heat coconut milk/ starch/ sugar blend until thickened. Cool. Put in freezer for a bit. When it's pretty thick, coat popsicle sticks in this stuff and set on plastic wrap in freezer, then after a while coat again.

Place the orange juice mixture into popsicle molds about half full, and it will be lying there, wide to receive. Then insert a coated stick in each and freeze until frozen to your liking.

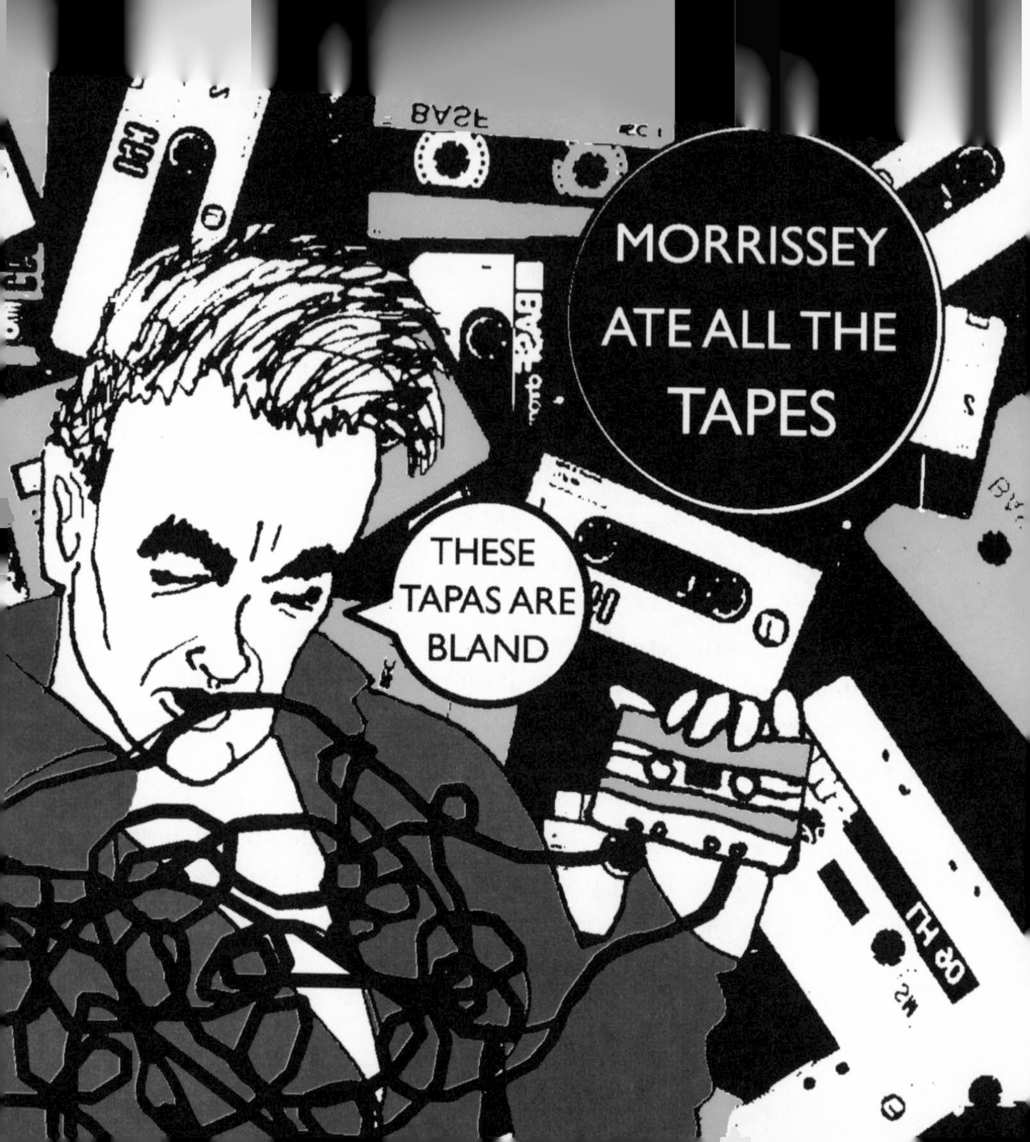
MORRISSEY ATE ALL THE TAPES
THESE TAPAS ARE BLAND

TAPAS

2 garlic cloves, minced

A couple small sprigs rosemary

½ teaspoon chili flakes

½ cup vegan cream cheez

2 tablespoons Italian parsley, minced

2 red bell peppers

1 cup olives, favorite types mixed

Several tablespoons olive oil

1 teaspoon balsamic vinegar

¼ cup sweet wine

1 pound radishes, split

Salt and pepper, to taste

1 red onion, thinly sliced

1 pound baby beets, peeled and quartered

¼ cup red wine vinegar

1 teaspoon coriander, crushed

1 teaspoon dry dill

¼ cup broth

Toss olives with rosemary, balsamic vinegar, ¼ teaspoon red pepper flakes, minced garlic clove, salt and pepper to taste, and set aside for a flavor up (you should probably add a little olive oil). Toss them every once in a while, seasoning more to taste.

Simmer red wine vinegar, a little garlic, the red onion, coriander, dill, broth, sweet wine, chili flakes, and salt and pepper to taste for 10 minutes. Add beets and radishes. Cover and simmer for 5 to 10 minutes, stirring here and there. Leave cover on and turn off heat. Set in fridge to cool.

Roast bell peppers at 400 degrees right on the rack for 20 to 30 minutes, or until they start to blacken. Place in a paper bag. After a little while, peel them, seed, and cut into strips. Mix cream cheez with parsley, salt, and a little pepper (maybe a bit of garlic), and roll dollops of that up in your pepper strips. Drizzle with a little oil, vinegar, and parsley before serving.

These are three simple tapas. I can't pretend it gets easier. Serve them together.

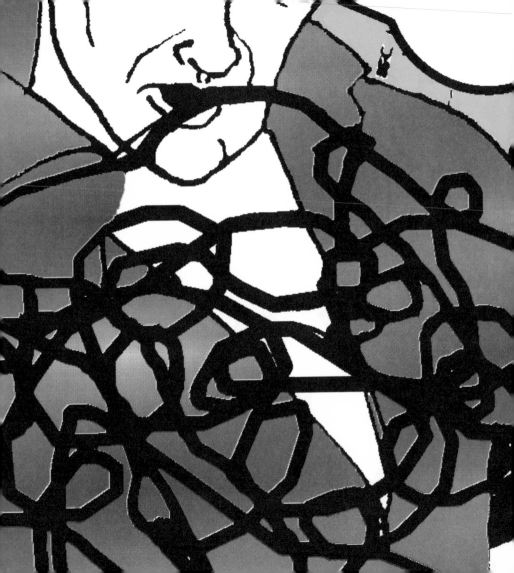

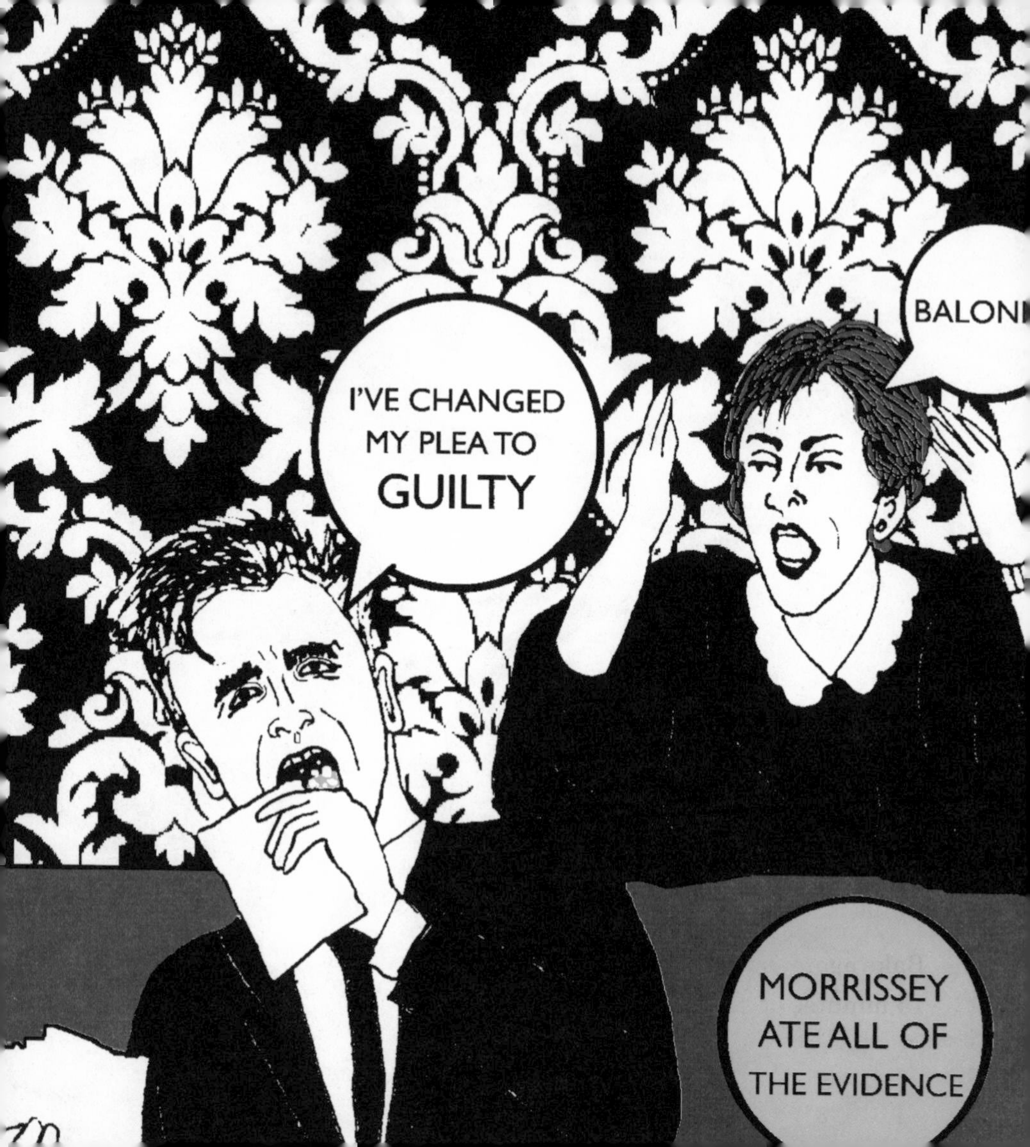
I'VE CHANGED MY PLEA TO GUILTY
BALON
MORRISSEY ATE ALL OF THE EVIDENCE

VEGAN BOLOGNA

1 pound firm tofu
1 teaspoon peppercorns, chopped
2 teaspoons paprika
1 teaspoon coriander
½ teaspoon cumin
2 tablespoons minced onions
2 cloves garlic, minced
3 or 4 tablespoons oil
1 cup broth
½ teaspoon ground annatto
Salt and pepper, to taste
Soy sauce, to taste

Slice tofu thinly and place in a baking dish. Cover with mixture of broth, paprika, annatto, soy sauce, salt and pepper, cumin, coriander, and garlic. Allow to sit for an hour or two, turning once.

Bake at 350 degrees for an hour, or until much of the liquid cooks off. Drain. Set on paper towels or a board, dot with onion and chopped peppercorns, sprinkle with salt, and place a weight on top to press those things gently, but insistently, into the tofus. Don't fret too much about them splitting. It's a miracle you've even made it this far.

Bake again, basting with some paprika, soy sauce, and oil for 10 to 15 minutes or so until done to your liking.

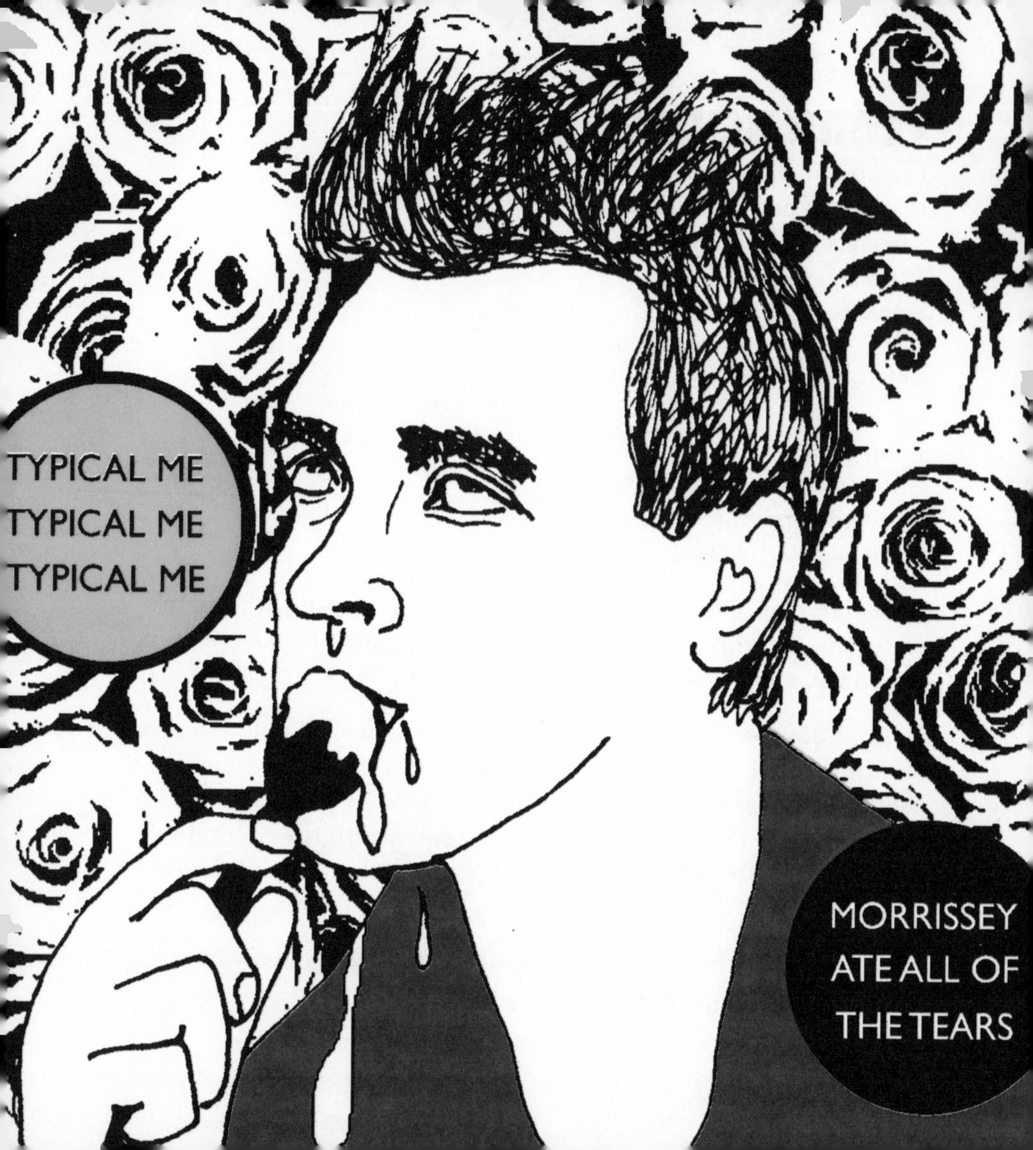
TYPICAL ME
TYPICAL ME
TYPICAL ME
MORRISSEY
ATE ALL OF
THE TEARS

TEARS

Salt
Soda
Grapefruit juice
Vodka
Ginger syrup
Lemon

In a shaker, mix two parts vodka, one part grapefruit juice, and ginger syrup to taste. Shake with ice.

Pour into salt-rimmed martini glass. Finish with a splash of soda and float a lemon slice in there. Have a drink and join me, join me, join me. I'm certain I heard you cry.

This is how my tears taste at least.

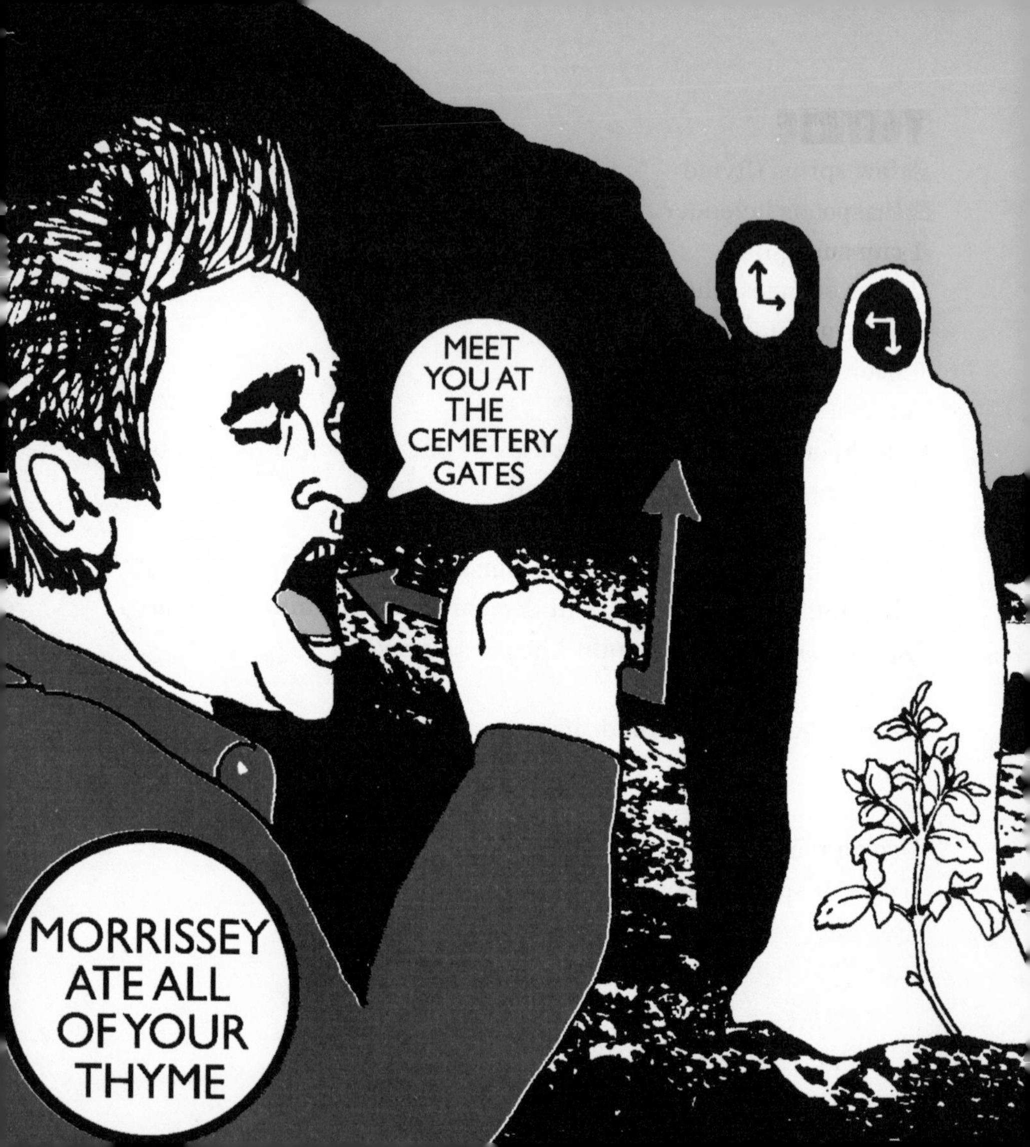
MEET YOU AT THE CEMETERY GATES
MORRISSEY ATE ALL OF YOUR THYME

THYME

A few sprigs thyme

2 teaspoons lavender flowers, in a little tied cloth bag or infuser

1 cup sugar

2 cups oranges, chopped

½ cup juice (apple or orange)

1 tablespoon oil

A pinch of salt

½ teaspoon vanilla

1 cup apples, peeled and chopped

Simmer all but vanilla in a pot for 15 to 20 minutes, stirring/whisking occasionally. Try to mash up that fruit. Add more liquid if there's not enough.

Remove lavender bag and thyme sprigs. Add vanilla. Mash and cool.

Use on toast or biscuits, which will cheer you up, and I haven't seen you smile in a while.

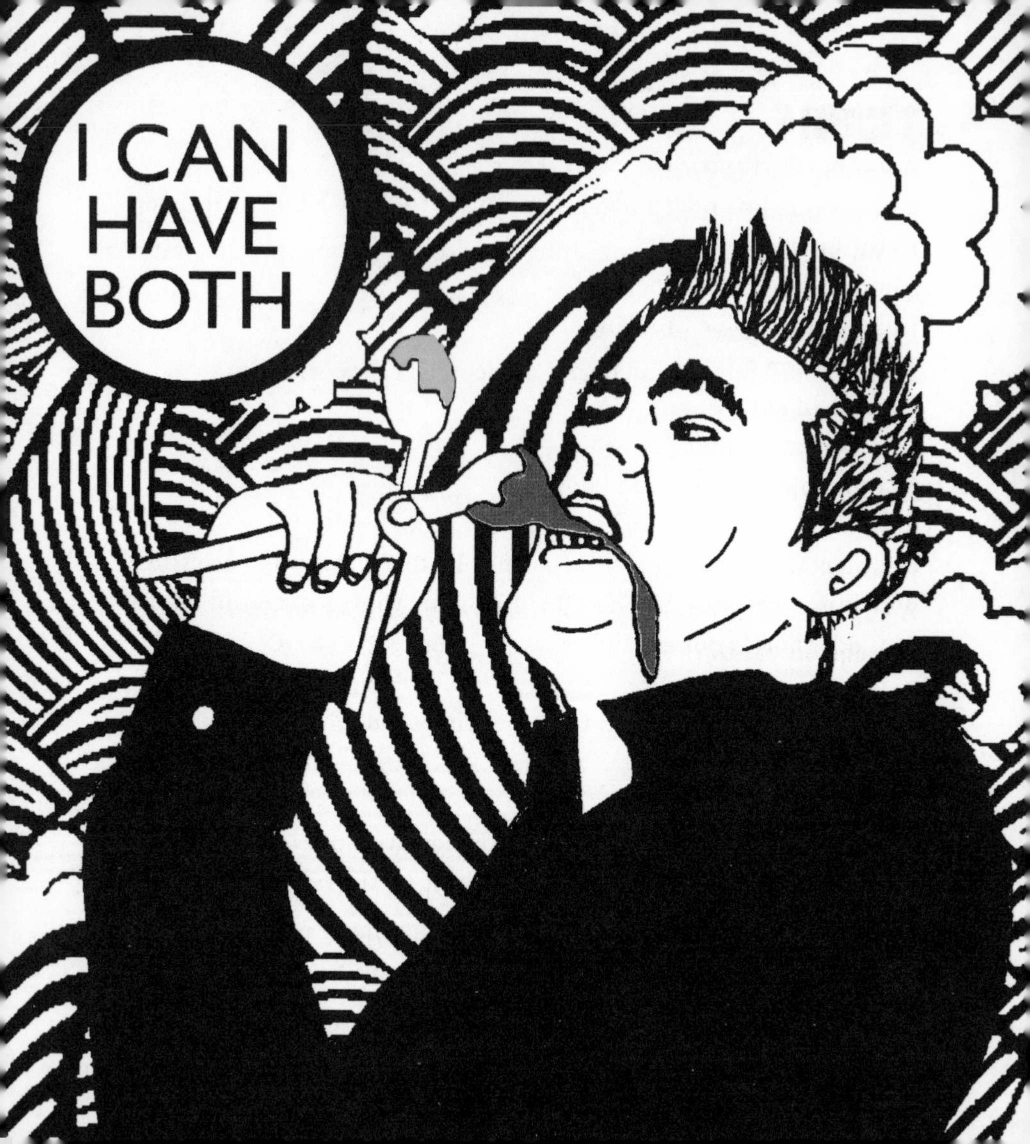
I CAN HAVE BOTH

BOTH

Strawberry spread:

½ cup chopped strawberries

1 cup vegan cream cheez, tofu or coconut cream (fix up with lemon juice)

1 teaspoon lemon juice

3 or 4 tablespoons strawberry, apricot, or raspberry jam

Salt and sugar, to taste

Chocolate spread:

½ cup cocoa (more if needed)

¼ cup oil or margarine

½ cup peeled hazelnuts (soak them overnight, then drain)

1 teaspoon vanilla

Salt, to taste

½ cup powdered sugar

A pinch or two of nutmeg

Vegan creamer as needed

Blend stuff for strawberry spread, and then chill. Blend stuff for chocolate spread, and then chill. Don't just hang around til you can be enticed inside, now you can have both!

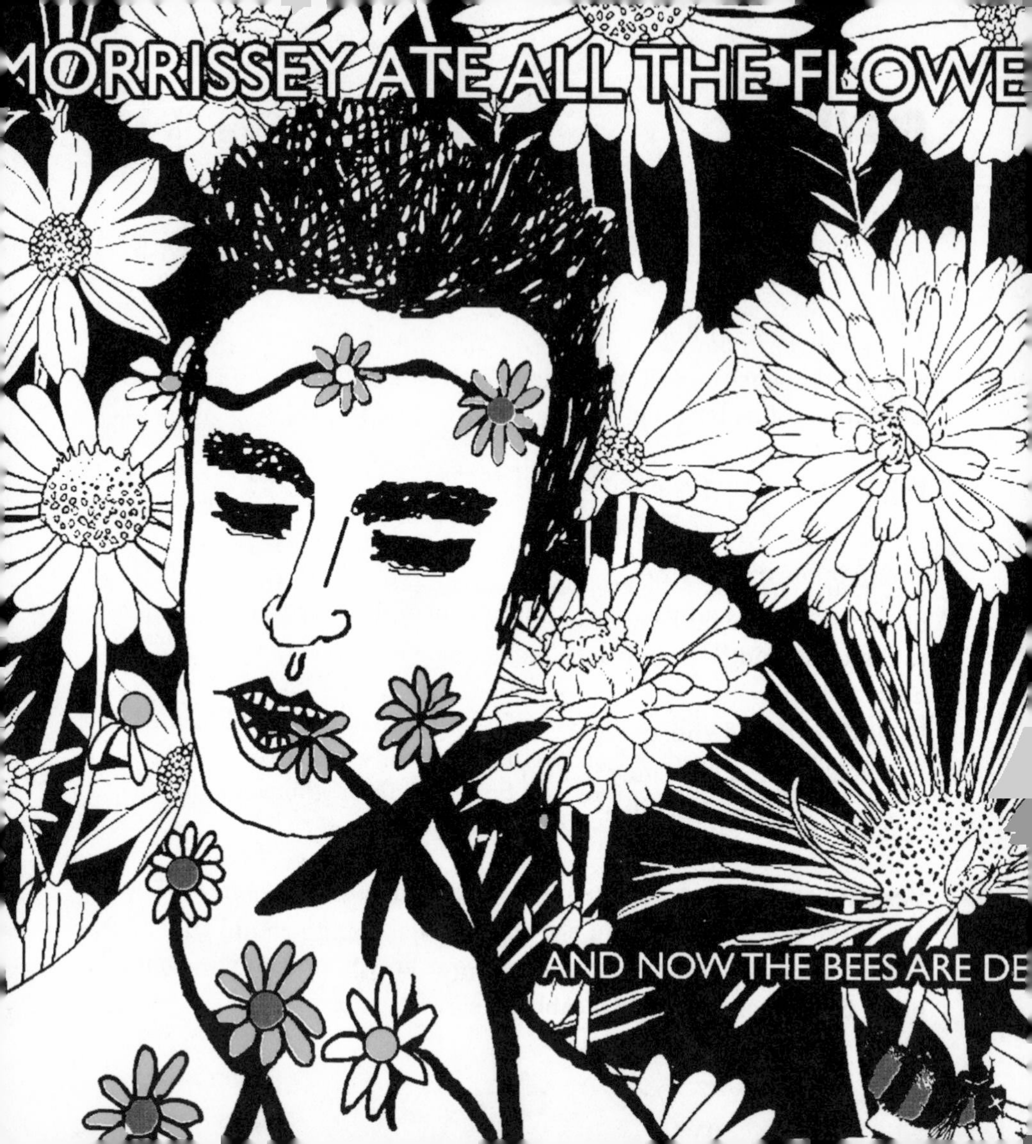

MORRISSEY ATE ALL THE FLOWE
AND NOW THE BEES ARE DE

FLOWERS

6 squash blossoms
$1/_3$ cup rice flour
$1/_3$ cup cornmeal
Salt and white pepper, to taste
½ teaspoon turmeric
1 teaspoon chili powder
A couple tablespoons oil, plus some for frying
1 or 2 teaspoons lemon juice
1 teaspoon garlic powder
½ teaspoon baking powder or soda
Broth or soy milk to make a batter (½ cup or more)

Mix flour, cornmeal, spices, lemon juice, powder, a little oil, and broth together to make a nice tasty batter, using salt or seasonings to taste. Should be pretty light like a crepe batter.

Dredge blossoms in this, and then fry, turning once, until browned and crispy on both sides. Don't spill the oil and cause fire—you'd be the first away because you're that type, and then who would finish making these?

You could additionally coat them in seasoned bread crumbs.

Serve with some green salsa and veg sour kreem, and maybe some black beans, tortillas, and a cabbage slaw.

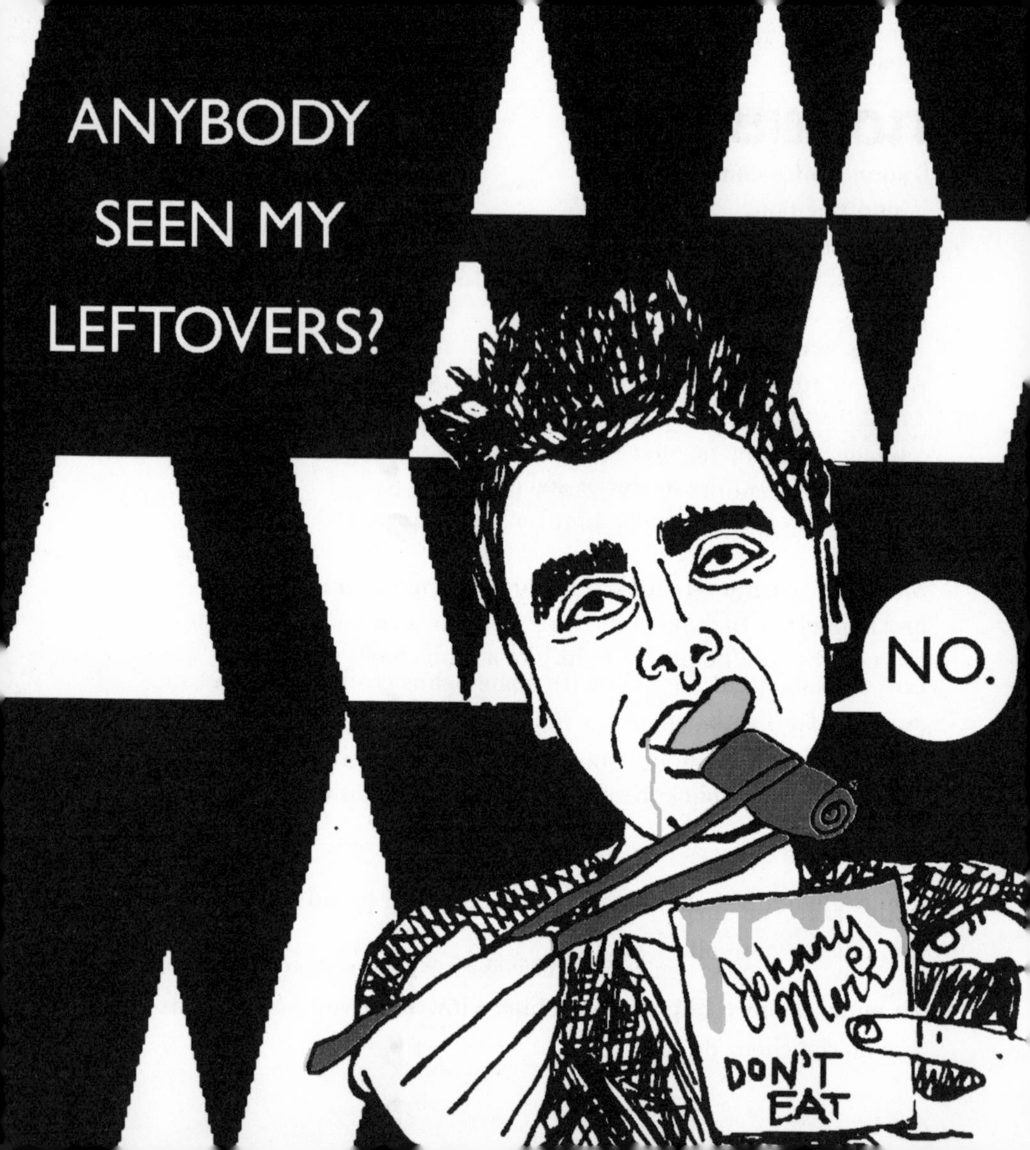
ANYBODY SEEN MY LEFTOVERS?
NO.
Johnny Marr
DON'T EAT

LEFTOVERS

Cheezy sauce or uncheez
Bread
Spaghetti or pizza sauce
Chopped veggies
Herbs
Spices
Broth, soup, or gravy
Chili or beans

Really, the amounts don't matter particularly.
After a spell, you might have these lying around.

Saute the veggies in a little oil, adding some salt and pepper, herbs, and spices.

Lay these in a baking dish with some beans/chili, spaghetti sauce, and a little broth or soup. Dot or drizzle with uncheezy sauce. Crumble bread and mix it with some spices, oil, and salt and pepper. Sprinkle over this casserole concoction.

Bake at 375 degrees for 40 minutes.

Voila! Leftover surprise. How does it taste? Well, why don't you find out for yourself.

To make it more like rarebit, start with the bread on the bottom and do the cheez on top.

EXISTENCE IS ONLY A GAME

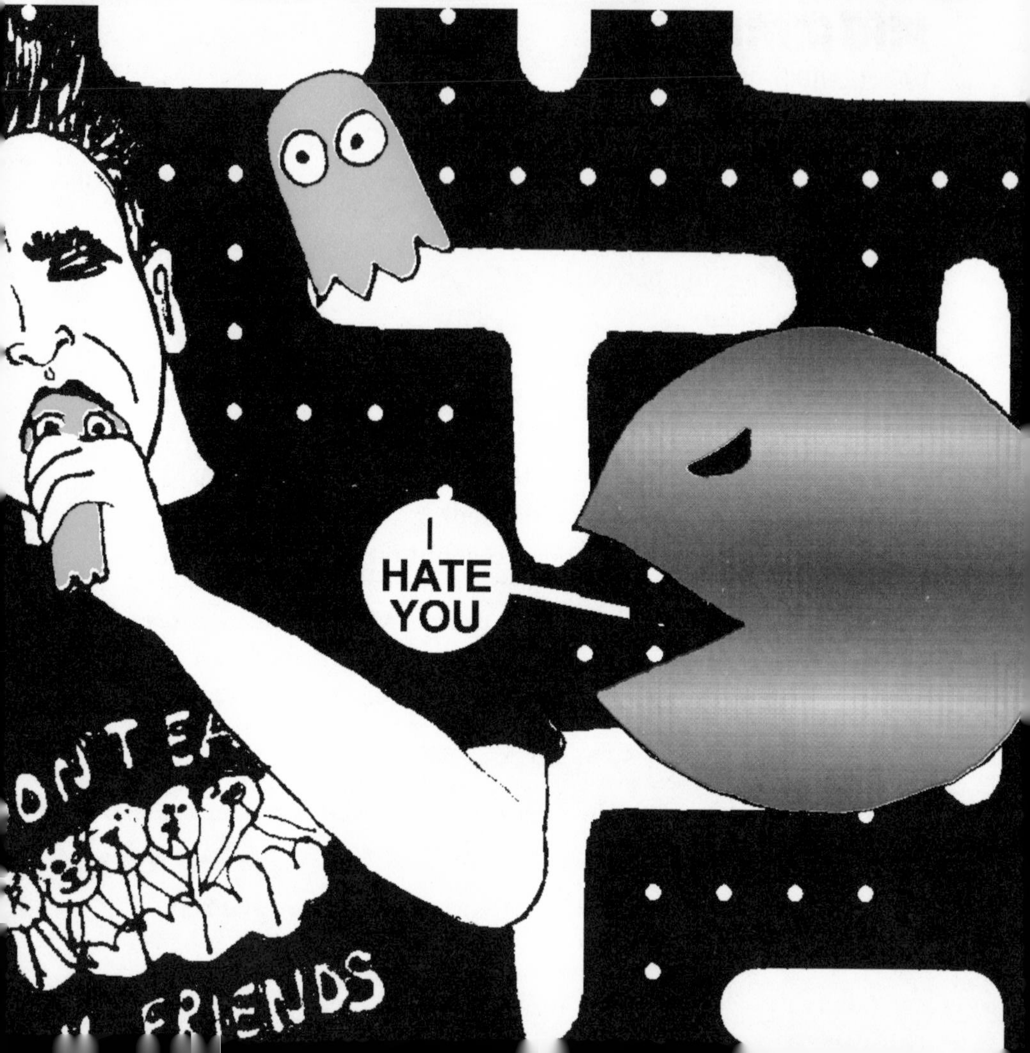
I HATE YOU
FRIENDS

PACMAN CAKE

1 ½ cup flour

½ cup sugar

¼ cup oil

½ cup soy or coconut milk

A pinch or two of salt

1 ½ teaspoon baking powder

¼ cup lemon juice

1 tablespoon lemon zest, grated

1 teaspoon vanilla

1 teaspoon turmeric or use a little yellow food coloring

Cloudberry jam (just get a jar; it's expensive but you're posh)

1 cup powdered sugar (more if needed)

2 to 3 tablespoon(s) margarine or coconut oil

2 to 3 tablespoon(s) lemon juice

A little soy milk if needed

A little turmeric or yellow food coloring

A pinch of salt

Mix dry cake ingredients, then add in wet. Bake in greased/floured 8-inch round cake pan at 350 degrees for 40 minutes or until done, my dear.

Take it out and turn the bugger out on a wire rack after a few minutes. Split into two layers. Next, cut a little pie slice out of it and get rid of that. See where this is going?

Spread cloudberry jam with a little lemon juice on the bottom layer, put the top back on. Mix the remaining ingredients together, adjusting amounts as required, and taste to make most delicious lemony frosting. You want it to be yellow as well, needless to say. Frost the cake once it cools. Cold hand, ice man. Oh look, it's Pacman!!

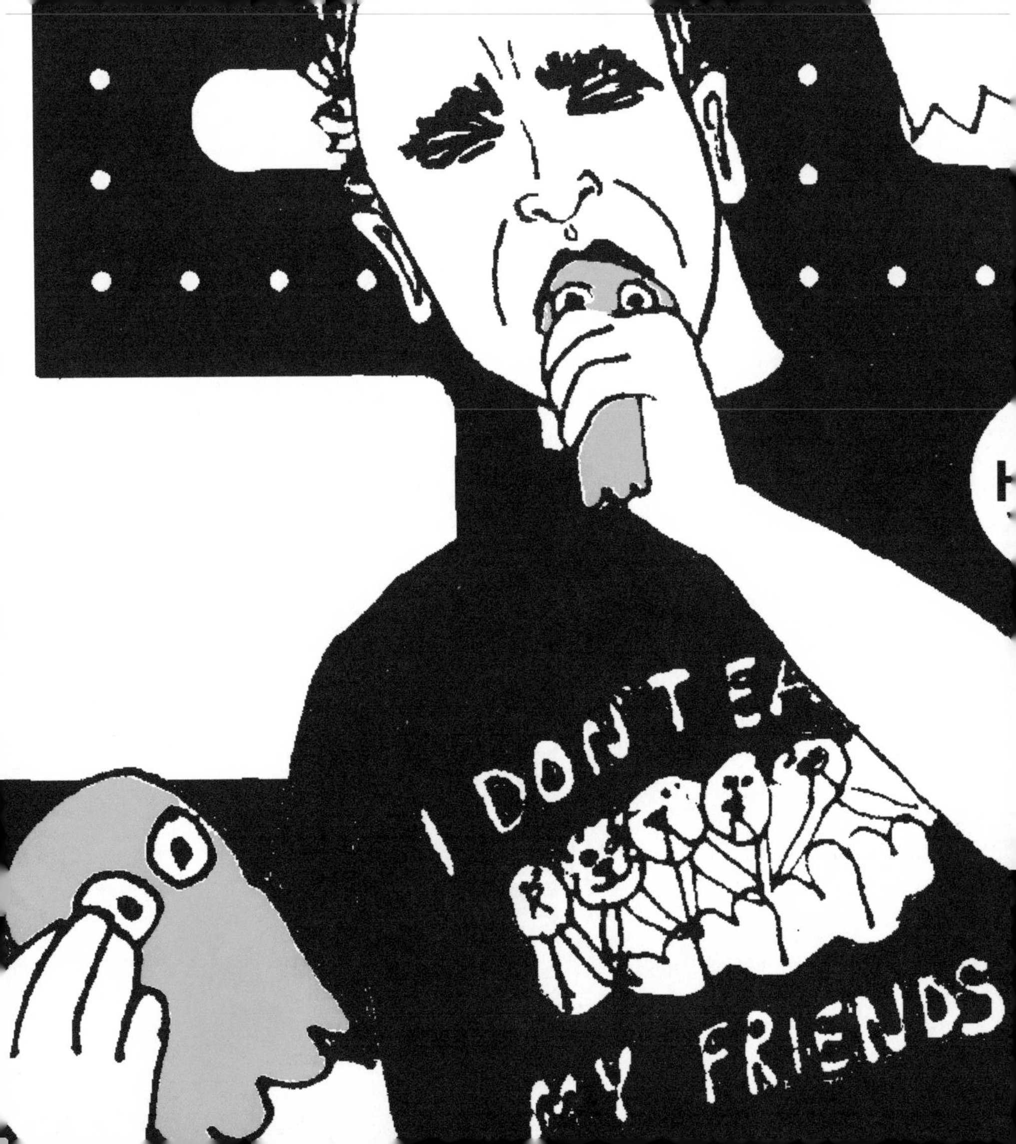
I DON'T EA
MY FRIENDS

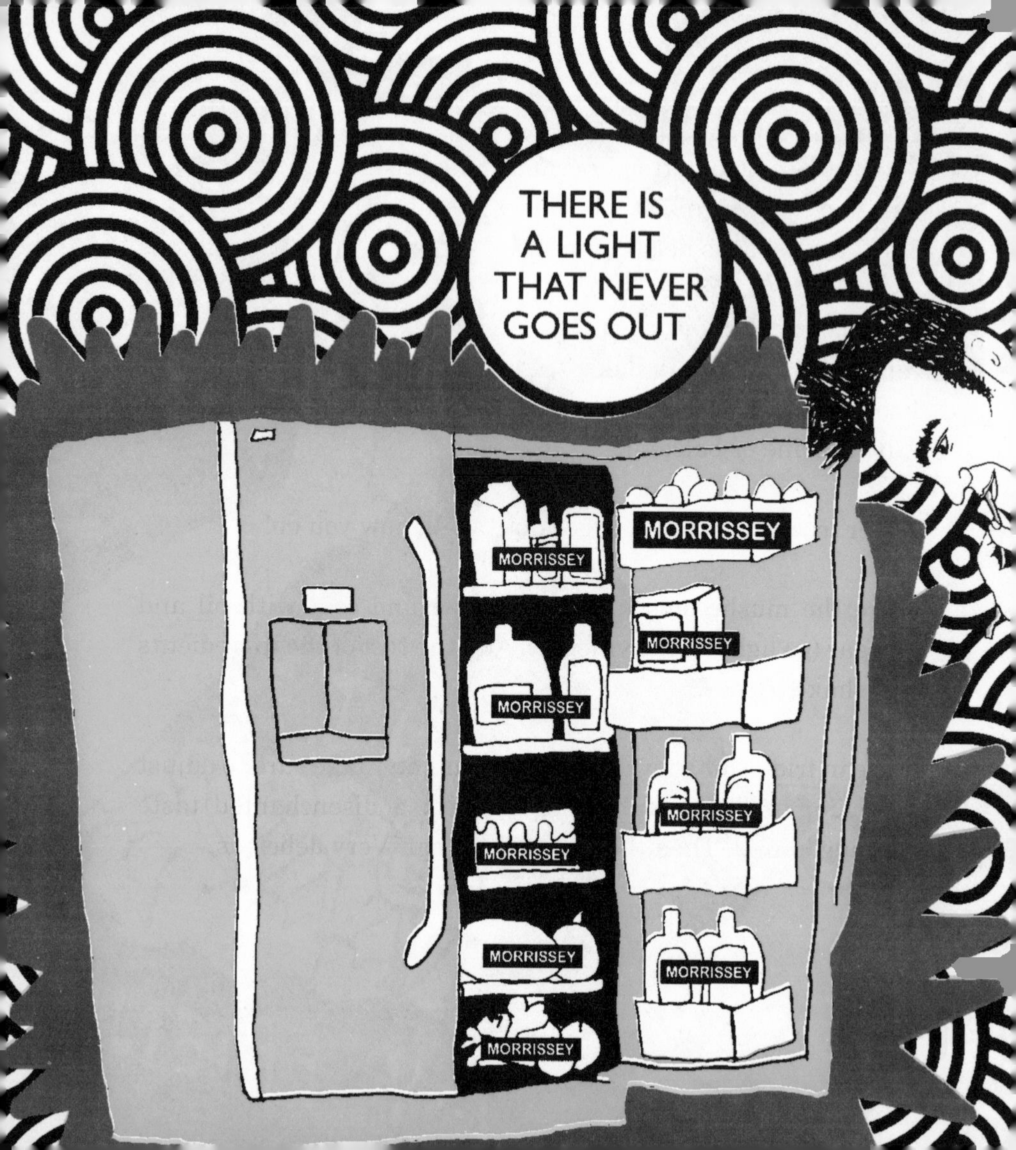
THERE IS
A LIGHT
THAT NEVER
GOES OUT
MORRISSEY
MORRISSEY
MORRISSEY
MORRISSEY
MORRISSEY
MORRISSEY
MORRISSEY
MORRISSEY
MORRISSEY
MORRISSEY

REFRIGERATOR

2 to 3 cups whole button or crimini mushrooms

Salt and pepper, to taste (be fairly liberal with the salt)

2 to 3 tablespoons herbs, minced

3 garlic cloves, minced

1 teaspoon chili powder

A pinch or two of chili flakes

1 to 2 teaspoons oil

A little brine or balsamic

Never "cooked" in the refrigerator? Well, now you do!

Place the mushrooms in a plastic bag and coat with oil and vinegar (go light on the vinegar). Add the rest of the ingredients and shake to coat.

Place in fridge for a few hours or overnight. Make sure to adjust seasonings so you don't wind up with a disenchanted taste running 'round. Then they're ready to eat. Very delicious.

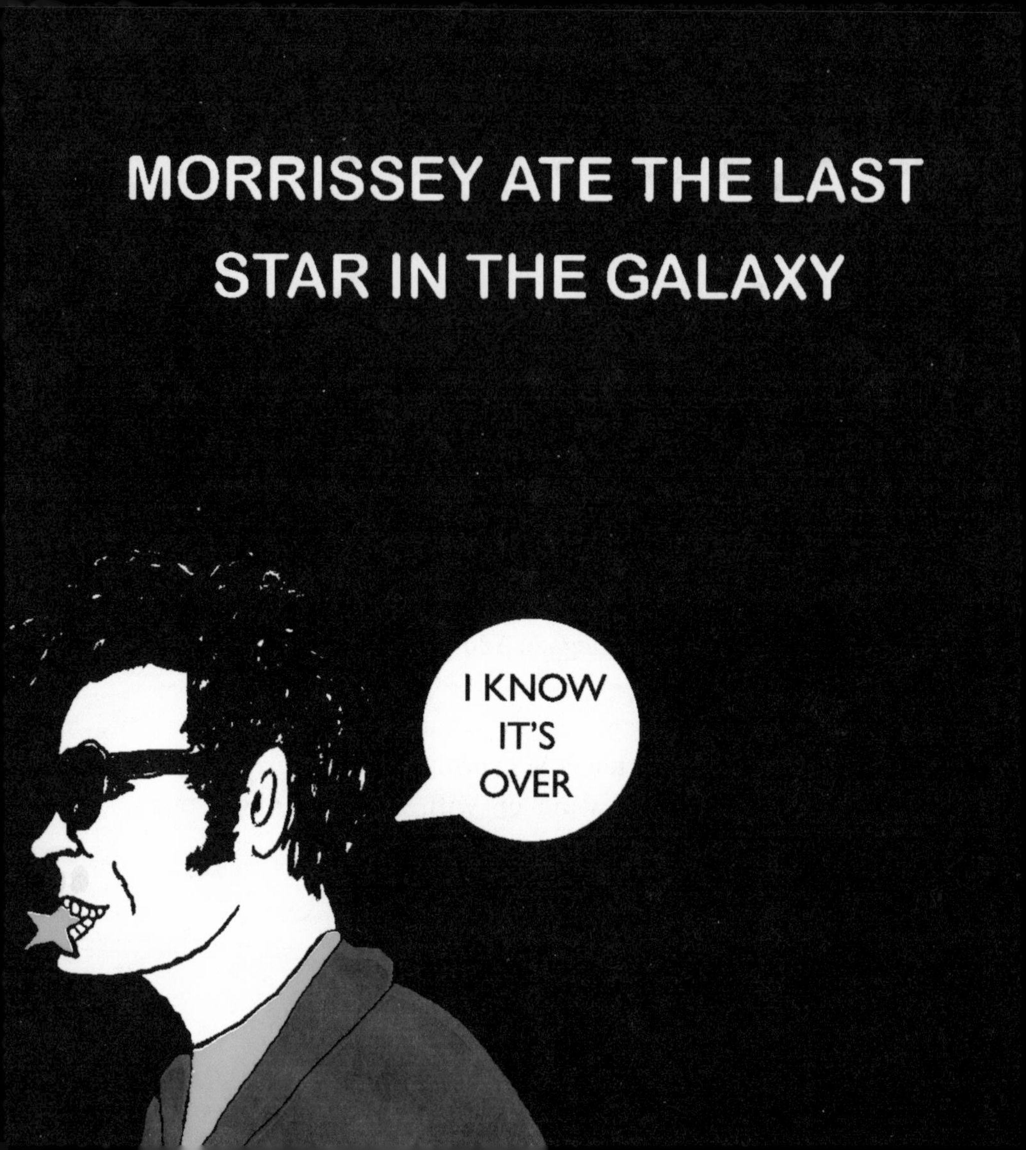
MORRISSEY ATE THE LAST STAR IN THE GALAXY
I KNOW IT'S OVER

STARS

4 star-shaped baking cups

Star cookie cutter (or just cut the stuff yourself)

Root vegetables and/or zucchini, thinly sliced (enough to make several layers)

½ cup tomato sauce (more as needed)

6 to 8 cloves garlic

2 tablespoon(s) herbs (basil, oregano, and sage are nice), minced

2 to 3 tablespoons red wine

¼ cup basil

½ cup pine nuts

1 tablespoon lemon juice

¼ cup olive oil

¼ cup cooked white beans or tofu

Salt and white pepper, to taste

2 tablespoons white miso

½ cup soy milk or other

2 tablespoons flour or rice flour

Cut the veggies into star shapes, of course (you have never been in love until you've seen the stars). The amount you use will depend on the size of your baking cups, or use one huge pan.

Blend tomato sauce with wine, 2 garlic cloves, herbs, and salt and pepper to taste. Set aside (adjust seasonings as you like; chopped mushrooms, peppers, or olives can also be good).

Blend half the olive oil, lemon juice, basil, pine nuts, 3 or 4 garlic cloves, and salt and white pepper to taste. Adjust seasonings as you please.

Blend white beans, flour, soy milk, rest of the oil, any remaining garlic, salt to taste, and a little white pepper. You can add vinegar, lemon juice, or nooch to this to jazz it up if you like. Or tahini (that's nice too).

Layer in each of the star pans (grease them): vegetables and the three sauces, in a different order for each little pan. You want a different layer on the top or bottom for each one, y'see!?

Bake at 375 degrees for 35 minutes, or until done to your liking.

If you can flip them out onto plates, do so, each should be a different color on the top. And also star shaped, LOL.

This is indeed a variation of a hot dish, if you thought it might be.

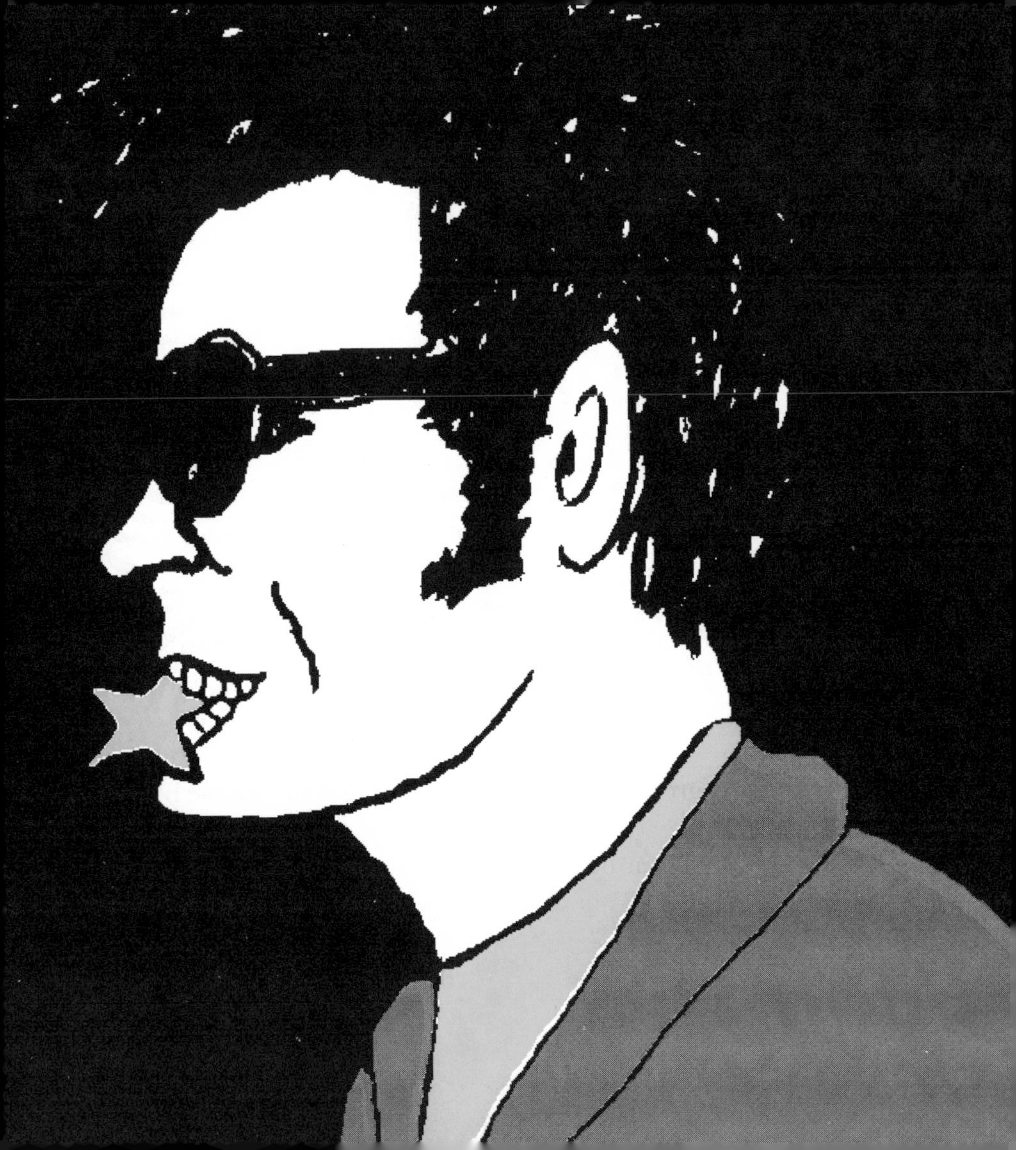

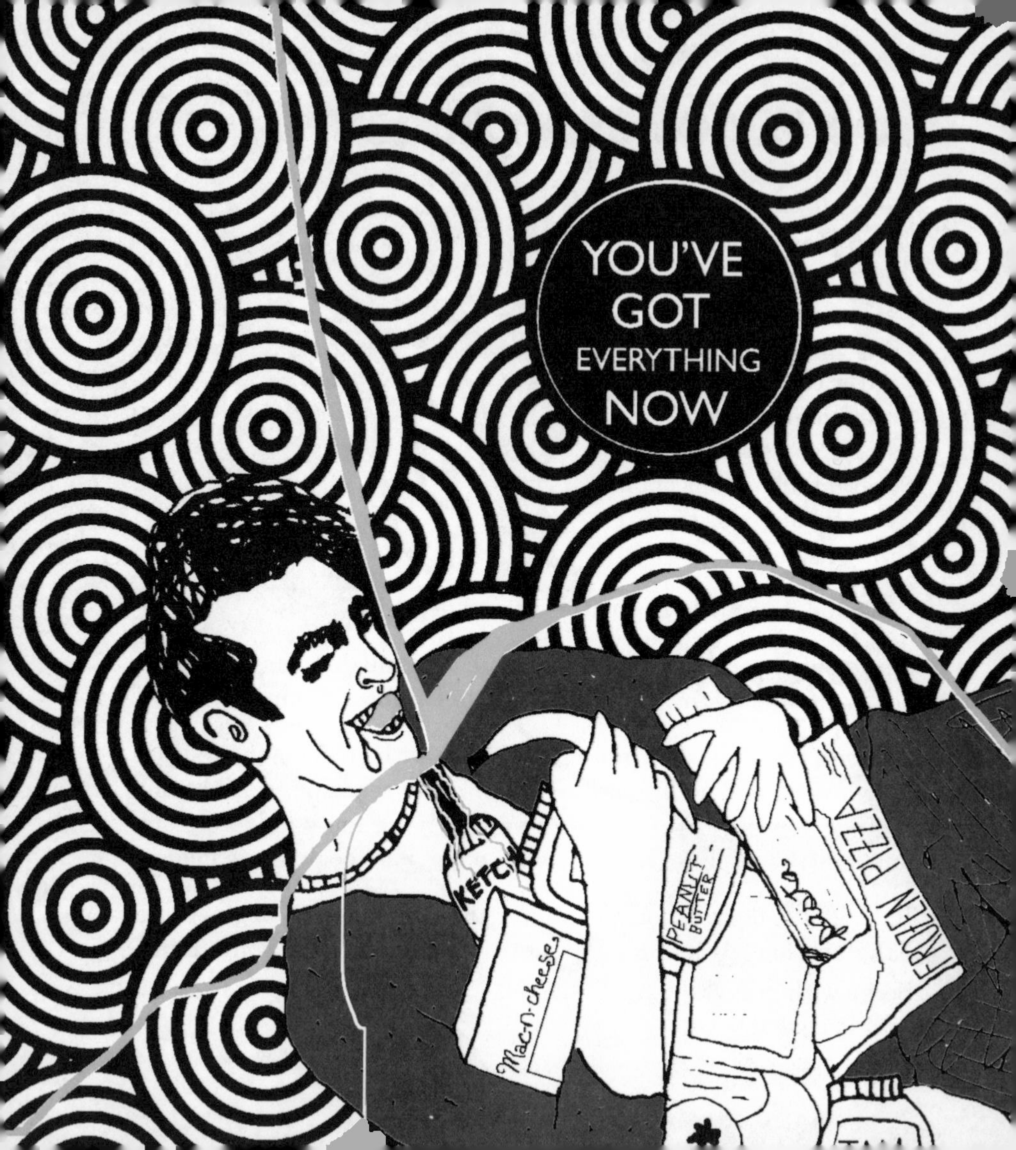
YOU'VE GOT EVERYTHING NOW
KETCH
Mac-n-cheese
PEANUT BUTTER
FROZEN PIZZA

YOU'VE GOT EVERYTHING

Bag of tater tots
1 cup wild rice
½ cup vegan cheez
1 cup vegan sour kreem
1 ½ cup chopped mushrooms
1 cup onions, diced
2 garlic cloves
½ pound green beans
Salt and pepper, to taste
Several tablespoons of oil
2 or 3 tablespoons tamari
Broth, as needed

Cook and drain wild rice with salt and pepper to taste.

Saute onions and garlic in a little oil. Add mushrooms and green beans, and then stir, seasoning to taste for about 5 minutes.

Grease a casserole dish and mix wild rice with green bean mixture, sour kreem, and additional tamari or other seasonings. Add some broth if you like. Sprinkle with vegan cheez, top with tater tots, and lightly salt. Take it all in; what a horrible mess you've made.

Bake at 425 degrees for 20 minutes then lower to 350 degrees and bake another 20 minutes, or until tots are done to your liking. Serve with gravy?

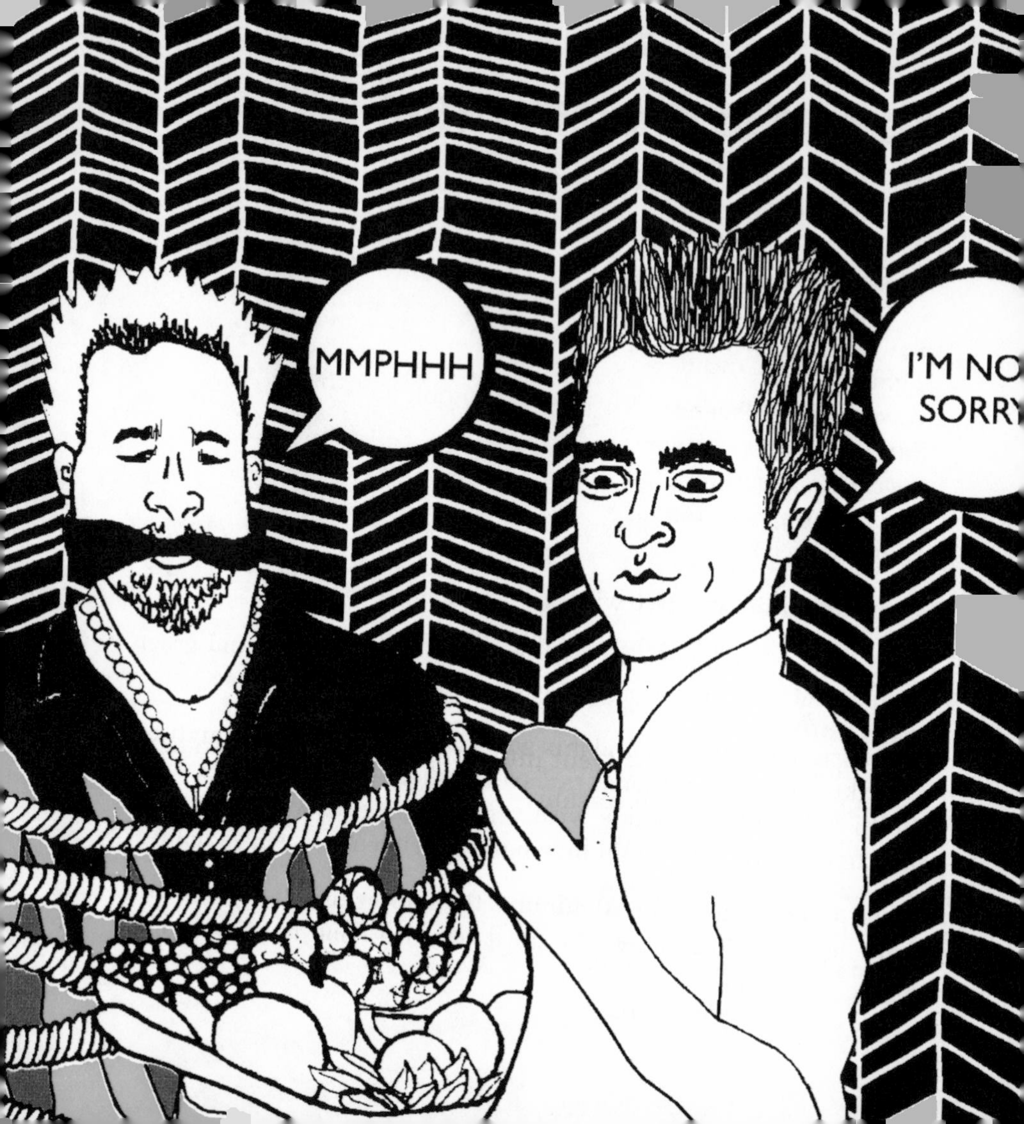
MMPHHH
I'M NO
SORRY

GUY FIERI

8 large wonton or egg-roll wrappers

Oil for frying

For jicama mango salsa:

1 cup jicama, small diced

½ cup mango, diced

1 ½ teaspoon tajin, or other seasoning blend

¼ cup tomatoes, diced

2 tablespoon(s) lime juice

Salt and pepper, to taste

¼ cup red onion, minced

2 garlic cloves, minced

2 or 3 tablespoon(s) cilantro, minced

For unfish:

1 pound tofu or taro root, cut into 8 thick strips (peel taro first)

1 tablespoon prepared wasabi

1 tablespoon sesame oil

1 or 2 tablespoon(s) sugar

¼ cup soy sauce

Nori sheets, cut into strips

For sweet soy sauce:

½ cup soy sauce

1 tablespoon ginger, grated

1 tablespoon sesame oil

3 or 4 tablespoons brown sugar

For wasabi cream:

2 or 3 tablespoons prepared wasabi

1 tablespoon lemon juice

1 or 2 tablespoon(s) oil

Salt, to taste

3 or 4 garlic cloves, smashed and peeled

¼ cup tofu, or cooked white beans

$\frac{1}{3}$ cup cashew or other milk (more as needed)

1 tablespoon white miso

1 cup cashew or other milk blended with $\frac{1}{3}$ cup flour

Chili seasoning and salt, to taste

1 ½ cup seasoned panko (bread crumbs)

We have selected his "won-tacos" as the model monstrosity for this one. You probably shouldn't be eating something like this, but hey, it's your life to wreck your own way.

Marinate the tofu or taro in the items from its section except nori. Set aside.

Mix the ingredients for sweet soy sauce and simmer for 10 to 15 minutes, or until it thickens a bit. Set aside.

Blend wasabi cream ingredients and adjust seasonings to taste.

Next, fry the wontons, using tongs to turn the ends up like a taco (this could be a pain in the ass, so just deal with it). Drain on absorbent paper.

Wrap seaweed strips around tofu/taro, dip in flour mixture and panko, and then fry, turning until browned.

Now, make the taco. Serve with lime.

Oh, white cloud, white cloud I could choke myself to please you.

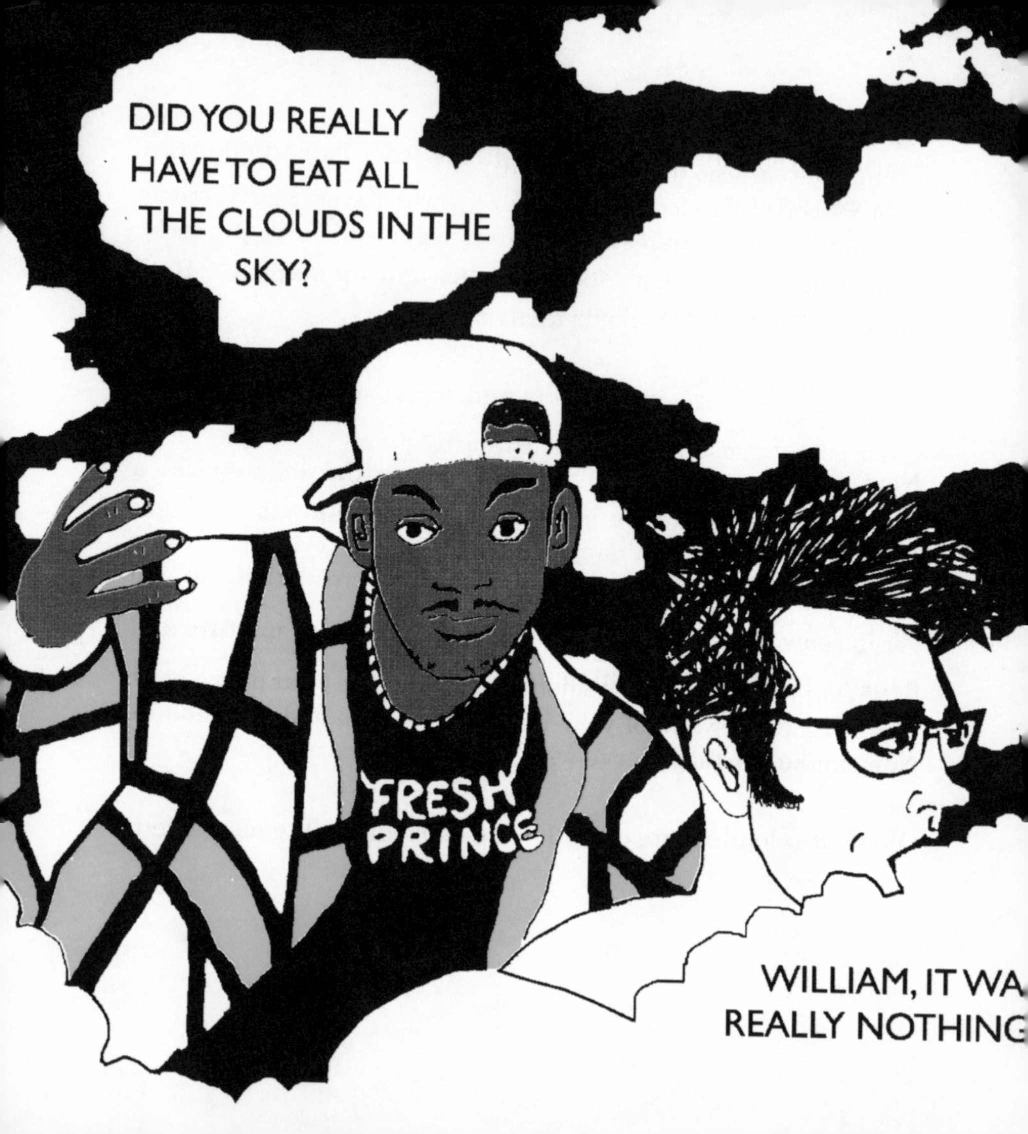
DID YOU REALLY HAVE TO EAT ALL THE CLOUDS IN THE SKY?
FRESH PRINCE
WILLIAM, IT WA
REALLY NOTHING

CLOUDS

¼ cup blue curacao (more if needed)

1 2-liter bottle of a clear soda in your favorite flavor (cherry, cream, or other fun uncoloured soda, any dyes will discolour your punch)

2 or 3 cups vodka

1 ½ cup vegan creamer (vanilla)

½ cup coconut cream

½ teaspoon vanilla

$^1/_3$ cup sugar

2 teaspoons cornstarch, or a little tapioca starch

2 tablespoons coconut oil

Blend soy creamer, vanilla, coconut cream, and cornstarch with a pinch salt and oil. Put in ice-cream maker and cream that shit. Put in freezer to set when ready.

Mix together the other ingredients, and place in a clear punch bowl. Place scoops or wafts of your ice cream in this, and then admire from various angles.

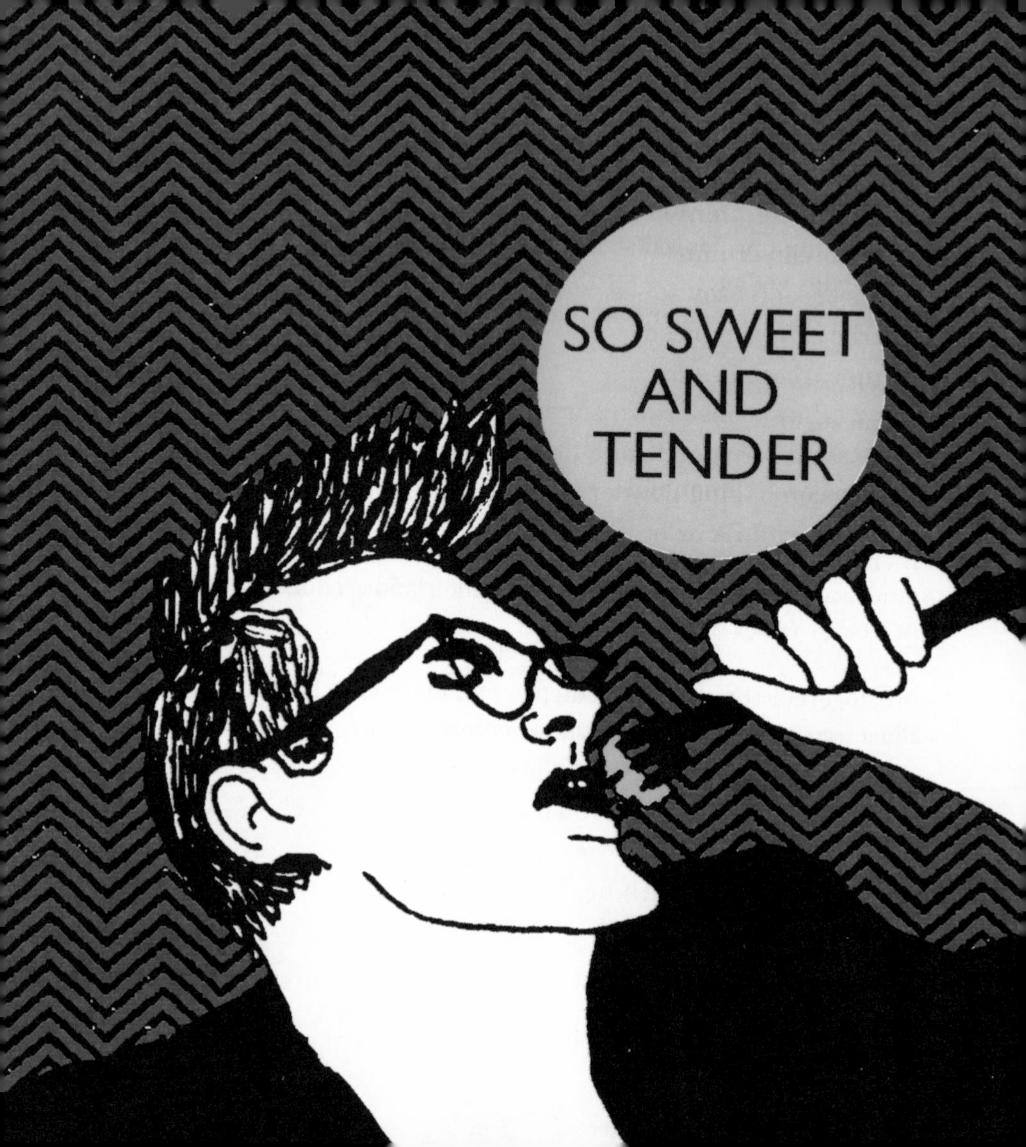
SO SWEET
AND
TENDER

SWEET AND TENDER

1 pound firm tofu

4 peach slices, thinly sliced

2 cups bread crumbs

2 tablespoon(s) soy sauce

2 garlic cloves, minced

¼ cup barbecue sauce

1 or 2 tablespoons brown sugar

1 cup flour

½ teaspoon baking powder

1 ⅓ cup soy milk or broth

Salt and pepper, to taste

1 teaspoon dried mixed herbs

Oil to fry (not a ton; it's not a deep fry)

Slice tofu into 4 slices. Sprinkle with soy sauce, coat in barbecue sauce, sprinkle with garlic cloves, place peach slice on top of each, and sprinkle with brown sugar. Set aside.

Mix bread crumbs with herbs and a little salt and pepper, and then place in a dish. Set aside.

Mix soy milk, flour, baking powder, salt and pepper to taste, and 2 tablespoons of oil. Add more liquid if needed (should be like a thin pancake batter). Take a brief moment to remember that in the midst of life, we are in death, etc.

Dip tofu and peach slices in the batter, making sure to keep each peach slice attached to the tofu. Dredge in bread crumbs and fry, turning once, until browned on both sides.

Good with peach or mango chutney, salsa, gravy (of course), marinara, sweet & sour sauce, etc.

Or lay the sweet and tender baby on a bed of kreemy garlic mashed potatoes and devour thems.

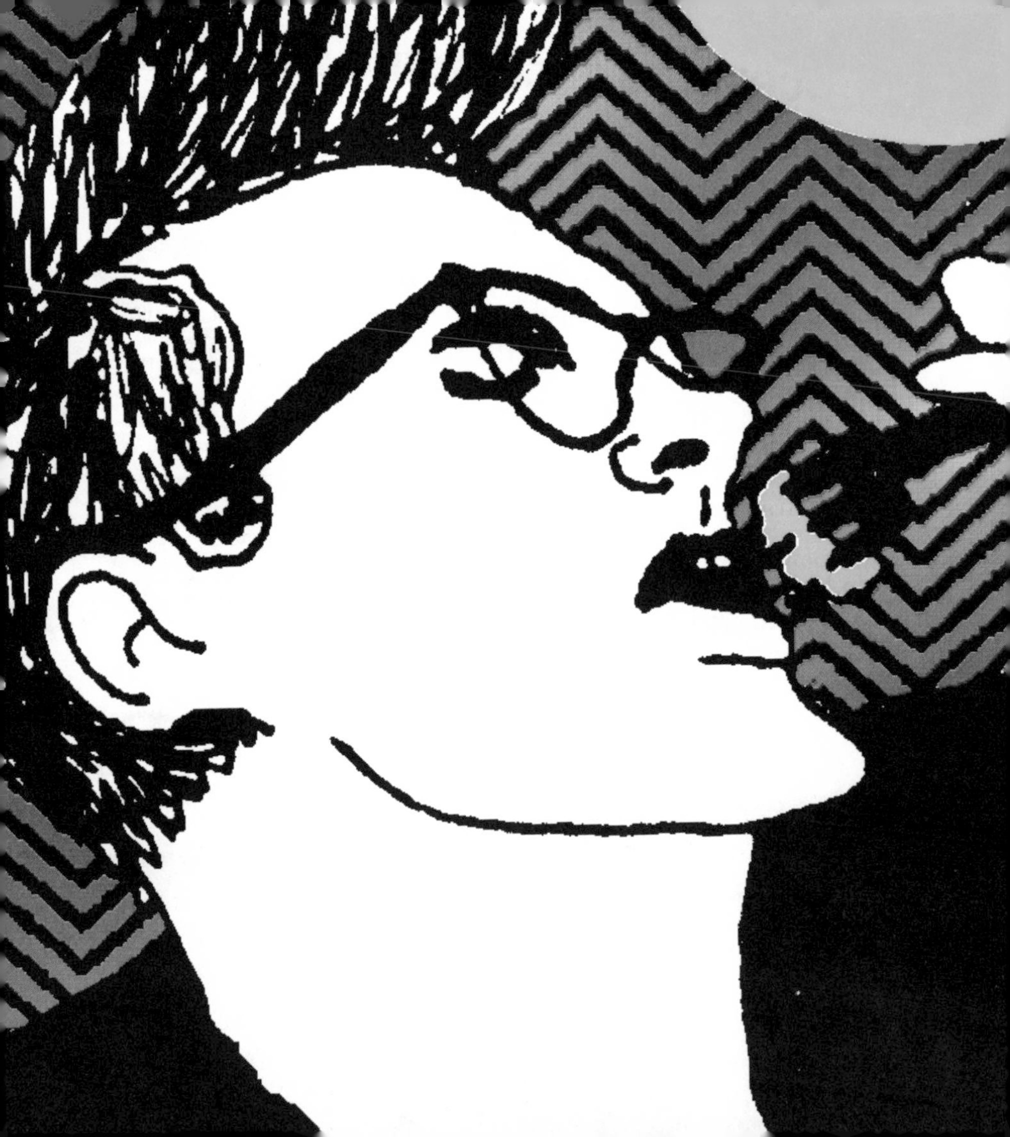

SUBSCRIBE TO EVERYTHING WE PUBLISH!

Do you love what Microcosm publishes?

Do you want us to publish more great stuff?

Would you like to receive each new title as it's published?

Subscribe as a BFF to our new titles and we'll mail them all to you as they are released!

$10-30/mo, pay what you can afford. Include your t-shirt size and month/date of birthday for a possible surprise! Subscription begins the month after it is purchased.

microcosmpublishing.com/bff

MORE WEIRD BOOKS FOR YOUR WEIRD FRIENDS:

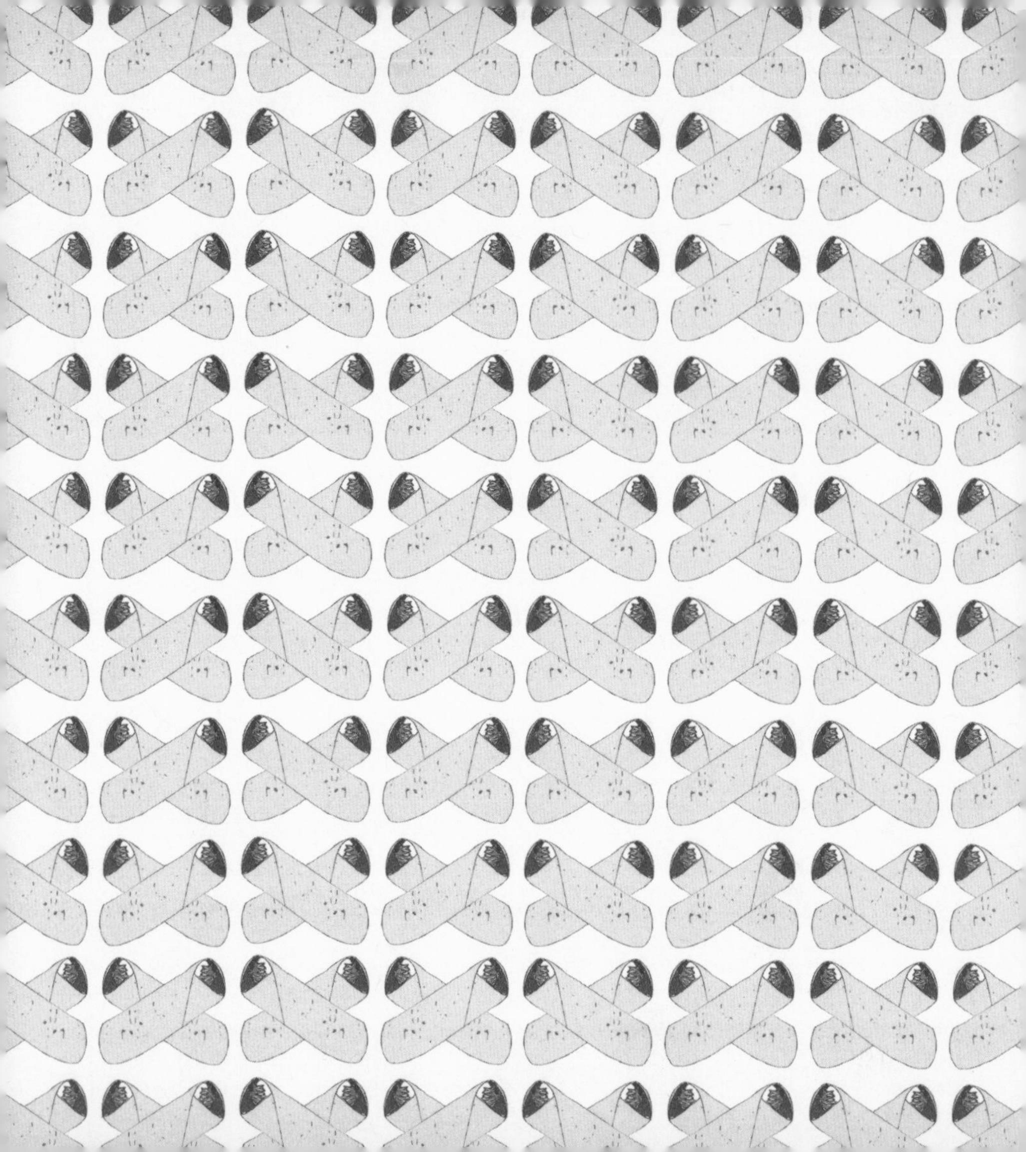